D0953483

10x6/14 25x5/18

HODA

How I Survived War Zones, Bad Hair, Cancer, and Kathie Lee

HODA KOTB

Simon & Schuster

New York   London   Toronto   Sydney

Simon & Schuster
1230 Avenue of the Americas
New York, NY 10020

First Simon & Schuster hardcover edition October 2010

SIMON & SCHUSTER and colophon are registered trademarks
of Simon & Schuster, Inc.

For information about special discounts for bulk purchases,
please contact Simon & Schuster Special Sales at
1-866-506-1949 or business@simonandschuster.com.

The Simon & Schuster Speakers Bureau can bring authors
to your live event. For more information or to book an event,
contact the Simon & Schuster Speakers Bureau at
1-866-248-3049 or visit our website at www.simonspeakers.com.

Designed by Nancy Singer

All photos courtesy of the author except *Saturday Night Live* stills, courtesy of NBC
Universal Photo Bank.
Permission to reprint "Brand New Day" lyrics courtesy of Joshua Radin;
"Anyway" lyrics courtesy of Alfred Music Publishing Co., Inc.

Manufactured in the United States of America

10   9   8   7   6   5   4   3   2   1

Library of Congress Cataloging-in-Publication Data

Kotb, Hoda.
    Hoda : how I survived war zones, bad hair, cancer, and Kathie Lee / Hoda Kotb.
       p.   cm.
    1. Kotb, Hoda, 1964–. 2. Television news anchors—United States—Biography.
3. Television journalists—United States—Biography. 4. Television personalities—
United States—Biography. I. Title.
    PN1992.4.K68A3 2010
    791.4502'8092—dc22
    [B]   2010012110

ISBN 978-1-4391-8948-1
ISBN 978-1-4391-8950-4 (ebook)

To Jim Lorenzini
For your endless inspiration

"If you want to make God laugh, tell him your plans."
This book is dedicated to anyone, like me,
who's made God bust a gut.

CONTENTS

INTRODUCTION

Recently, I was walking through one of New York City's terrific neighborhood street fairs teeming with colorful booths. Banners promised "Millions of Socks!" and vendors proudly displayed tie-dyed scarves and chocolate-covered marshmallows on skewers. The crowd had a Sunday pace and I happily relaxed into the mix of sun-soakers and serious shoppers. As I wandered, some who watch a bit of television offered their kind hellos as they passed by. A friendly guy selling piano lessons wanted to chat. He asked one of the two questions I most often hear.

One is, "Where are you from?"
He asked the other: "How did you get to where you are today?"

It's always that second question that makes me want to pull out a vinyl pocket photo file. It would flip-flop-flip all the way down to the ground, filled with pictures of the extraordinary people who guided me, who took a chance on me, who supported me. They are the answer. They are how I got to where I am today.

Think of all the people who'd fill *your* pocket photo file. Or even the pages of your book. I never really considered writing a book, and wondered—when someone suggested the idea—whether I could. I can't remember a damn thing! Big problem. A good friend of mine, aware of my recall issues, mailed me a package of dried blueberries when she heard about my book project. The enclosed card (I'm told) read, "Good for your memory. Start eating these by the bushel!" Well, the package never arrived. Classic. The berries got lost, just like my memories.

Turns out, though, several hundred pages later, I *did* have a book in me. I *do* remember things once I dig around in the fuzzy matter a bit. (I wisely issued shovels to my siblings, too.) So, what's my book about? It's about where I'm from. My family. The hunt for my first television job. And the double whammy that took my breast and broke my heart at the same time. It's about stories I've covered around the globe. Hurricanes Katrina and Kathie Lee. What I've learned so far in my life. It's about how the dirt that gets kicked in our faces sometimes transforms into magic dust. Most important, though, these pages are a way to give credit and thanks to the people who boldly stepped up when no one else would, and who quietly sat down next to me without being asked. My book is about all that and a random guy on a plane who told me, "Don't hog your journey."

Okay, I won't. Here's my journey. I'm so glad you're here. Pass the blueberries.

MY VINYL PHOTO FILE

Dad: Born and raised in Cairo, my dad came to America with my mom for a better life and to have a family. He raised me and my siblings as American kids, but we traveled to Egypt each summer to visit relatives and run our hands over the exotic pyramids. My dad valued learning and excellence, and his approval still drives me today. He died suddenly when I was in college—the most significant loss in my life.

Mom: Behind every strong woman is a stronger woman. That's my mom. Who I am and who I want to be is based on what I see in my mother. She's gutsy, game for everything, and is my inspiration to live life with a positive outlook. *And* she agreed to share her family recipe for baklava with you. Love her.

Hala: To know her is to do what she says. Hala's usually right and she's my big sister. Funny, smart, and loyal, Hala is the girl I want by my side and on my side. She was my rock when my world was rocked in 2007. I could not have made it through two of the biggest challenges of my life without my sister.

Adel: My brother is a husband and father now, but to me he'll always be the little kid Hala and I ordered around. The poor guy has been dominated by estrogen for decades, and now he has a wife and daughter along with the three Kotb women he's managed his entire life. Adel is perfect in the role—calm, patient, and hilarious. He is so many things I am not—and so much of what I look for in a good man.

Hannah: She's damn near perfect. What can I say? Hannah is Adel's daughter, my niece, and when "Aunt Hodie" comes out of her sweet mouth, I melt. She's the family's first and only of the next generation and she makes our world more fun. When I see Hannah's dark brown curls bobbing my way, I want kids even more.

Karen: Karen is my dearest friend and we talk on the phone every day, several times a day. The 200 miles between us may as well be zero. She lives in Boston, where she works as a morning TV anchor, but we met in New Orleans at WWL-TV. Both of our hearts broke covering Hurricane Katrina in 2005. I share with Karen a mutual love for that city and all the things that matter in my life.

Ex-Husband: I was divorced in 2008 after a two-year marriage. I won't dwell on this in the book. Too many other people deserve the ink.

Stan Sandroni: Who gave you your first real job? Stan gave me mine after I'd been rejected more than two dozen times. In 1987, I was driving around the Southeast in my mom's car, video résumé tape in my hand. Stan saw something in me that was invisible to twenty-seven other news directors who ejected my tape and said "Good luck." Stan hired me at WXVT-TV in Greenville, Mississippi, and gave me the start I needed in an industry that I love to this day.

Man on the plane: In 2007, I met a man somewhere over Ireland. I know his name, but when I tell his story, I call him "the man on the plane" because our meeting was so random and brief. Opposite of that was his memorable message—so specific and enlightening. He's an angel in my life whom I met soaring through the heavens, and who I initially thought was just a stranger sitting to my left.

Dr. Freya Schnabel: When I was diagnosed with cancer in 2007, I sought out the best surgeon in New York to tackle my cancer. She turned out to be Dr. Freya Schnabel. I love her solid reputation, calm demeanor, and sense of humor. I am forever grateful to her. When Freya found out I was writing a book, she made me promise to make her sound "blond and willowy." So, when you read about Dr. Schnabel, picture her as blond, willowy, and the best at what she does. I swear, it's all true.

Amy Rosenblum: Not everyone says things to your face that you may not want to hear, thank God. But in the case of Amy Rosenblum, you probably need to listen. She's a master at seeing people's strengths and weaknesses and that makes her a game changer. When she worked as a producer for the *Today* show, Amy helped me not only stay in the game, but advance a few spaces on the board. All the way to the fourth hour of *Today*.

Kathie Lee: Her name alone elicits a response—a smile or a groan. There's not much middle ground when it comes to people's reaction to Kathie Lee, but the middle is not where she hangs out. She's at home on one side or the other, with solid opinions about everything and a willingness to share them. If she's your good friend, she'll share everything else with you, too. I've come to know Kathie Lee as generous, loyal, and skilled in the art of good TV. In my wildest dreams I never thought I'd be sharing my mornings and several cocktails with KLG.

My hair: I make a big deal out of my hair in this book and you may think that's weird. But my life story would be incomplete without explaining the pain in the ass that is my frizzy, coarse mop. I've had to tangle with this lid my whole life—and you're gonna hear about it.

PART ONE

The Back Story

1

WHAT IS YOU?

There was a day in Greenville, Mississippi, that didn't really surprise me, but it did startle me. I was twenty-one, working as a television news reporter at the CBS affiliate, making a call on a pay phone. An older black woman walked up to me in the phone booth, cupped my face in her hands, looked into my eyes, and asked, "What is you?"

There it was. The question. People have asked it in one form or another for most of my life. Always, the answer in my head is: *I'm just me.* But I don't mind. I get that my name and my appearance require an explanation.

So, here it is.

I am Egyptian.

So is my name, Hoda Kotb.

What? Rhoda? Yoda Kotba? I've even had . . . *Photo Copy?*

My name has always triggered a guessing game. Is it pronounced Kotbeeeeee? Isn't there a vowel missing? *NBC Nightly News* anchor

With NBC's Brian Williams

Brian Williams once told me that I was the land mine in his tele-prompter. (Oh, Lord . . . here comes that name . . .)

Both of my parents were born in Egypt. And believe it or not, Hoda Kotb is actually the Jane Smith of the Nile. If you walk down the streets of Cairo and yell "Hi, Hoda!" a dozen girls will turn. Over there, I am every girl. Here, I'm unique. And I like that.

My parents, Sameha and Abdel Kotb, met at a law firm where they both worked after graduating from Cairo University in 1958. My dad, captain of a club crew team, invited a big group of female coworkers, including my mom, to watch him row in a race along the Nile River. He was already in a serious relationship with a girl from Germany, so his invitation was simply for fun.

Well, my mom was the only girl to show up on the banks of the river that day to watch my dad row, row, row his boat. And, as fate would have it, his sole spectator would soon become his soul mate.

He broke up with his girlfriend, the two families checked each other out, and in 1959, my mom and dad were married at an officers' club in Cairo, with the ancient Egyptian pyramids as a dramatic backdrop.

Egyptian weddings are a *big* deal. The hot-damn-I-think-I-see-a-sparkling-oasis-in-the-middle-of-the-Sahara kind of big. The goal is to dazzle, beginning with what's known in the Middle East as the *zaffa*. Picture a shimmering procession of belly dancers, musicians, and men carrying flaming swords. They signify with great splendor that a wedding is about to begin. In America, the next step would be the ceremony and the vows. But in Egypt, weddings unfold in the reverse order. The actual signing of the marriage papers comes right *before* the wedding, so the couple is already officially married by the time the ceremony begins. My parents' wedding did indeed follow the ancient tradition of *zaffa*, complete with a festive march of bagpipes, horns, and drums. Down came my mom from atop a long staircase, wearing a beautiful white gown hemmed at mid-calf, as was the Egyptian tradition during the time. My maternal grandfather was a Supreme Court judge in Egypt, so the guest list included quite a rock star—Egyptian president Gamal Abdel Nasser—and his cabinet members, too.

Loud and lively, the wedding celebration included an amazing buffet of traditional Egyptian food. There were several kinds of savory salads and saffron rice. Meat dishes featured kufta, kebabs, and grilled chicken along with fish. For dessert, in addition to a Western-style wedding cake, guests also were served baklava and other layered, honey-soaked pastries. The celebration lasted into the wee hours of the morning. The now Mr. and Mrs. Kotb stayed in Cairo for their honeymoon and enjoyed a room at the Mena House, a luxury hotel.

Only one week later, my parents departed for a new life in the United States. That fact alone proves that I come from strong, brave stock. If you could actually look at my family roots under a micro-

My grandfather Mahmoud Abdel-Latif; my great-aunt Moufida; my aunt Safi; Mom; President Nasser; Dad; my uncle Abdel Hamid; and pictured in the back, my grandmother Tawhida

scope, you'd see countless strands of rebar winding through the female side. So strong are the women before me, there are pioneers everywhere you look. My maternal grandmother, Tawhida, was a pistol. She became a doctor at a time when it was unheard of for women to assume such roles. And she was raising seven kids! My mom's aunt, my great-aunt Moufida, was the first female lawyer in all of Egypt back in the 1930s. She also became a member of parliament during that time, another difficult feat for a woman. And she achieved it all while raising nine kids! There's a story about how she bristled when a male lawyer barked at her, "You, get me some tea!" She refused, and said, "No. I'm a lawyer just like you." (No surprise that my own mother raised three children while she pursued a second degree and worked.)

At Cairo University, my father learned to speak four languages and walked away with bachelor's and master's degrees in petroleum engineering. My mom graduated first in her class and earned a law degree. So, why did they leave for the United States just a week after they were married?

For a very cool opportunity.

My father's top grades, followed by his very first engineering job in Germany, landed him a scholarship to get his Ph.D. at the University of Oklahoma, a world-renowned petroleum engineering school. My mom's law degree would not be recognized in the United States, but since she always loved books, she happily chose to study for a master's in library science also at the University of Oklahoma. Yep, Okies from . . . Cairo. (Doesn't quite have the same ring, does it?) There they were, in Norman, Oklahoma, both enrolled at OU, starting the family they'd always dreamed of and going to college. For extra money, my parents both interviewed for jobs at the state hospital. Whoops! Those two words—state hospital—didn't click in their culture as a facility for people with psychiatric issues. Understandably, my dad didn't last very long—none too happy about wrestling patients in the maximum security ward. My mom stayed for a year and a half, working as a nurse's assistant. On a brighter note, the Kotbs took in their first-ever football game in Norman, cheering on the Oklahoma Sooners and absorbing every detail about this very American sport—one they would come to love for life.

I recently watched home movies of my parents, living in Oklahoma and doing their thing. The films were made for the folks back home to show what 'A Day in the Life of the Kotbs in America' looked like. The reels show a classic scene—my dad in his hard hat at the Oklahoma oil rigs doing fieldwork for school. (Cue *Leave It to Beaver.*) He gets out of a shiny blue car, shuts the solid door, and walks off clutching his standard-issue lunch box. There are shots of him eating a sandwich, getting back into the car, then the film cuts to him and my mom holding hands and walking into the surf

Sami and Abdel Kotb

on Galveston Bay. What must all the relatives have thought of this young and brave couple!

Over four years, from 1961 to 1965, my parents had three kids—my sister Hala (pronounced Hala like Hala-fornia), me, and my brother Adel (rhymes with rattle). My parents were so proud to be Americans citizens. They dressed in the current styles and demanded we speak English as our first language. They wanted us to be red, white, and blue. We were United States citizens and were taught to never consider ourselves different. Imagine that! Me with my wild, frizzy hair, stop-sign glasses, and funny name. But still, we were reared as American kids. What a gift from my parents, raising us to never live in the shadow of "different."

Now, to be clear, I didn't *always* feel all-American. My looks often

Me in my stop-sign glasses,
sixth grade photo

left me feeling self-conscious. As much as my parents raised us to fit
in, I couldn't whitewash my name or this hair. God, this hair. (More
about that later and often.) By the time I was old enough to go to
kindergarten, we had moved from Oklahoma to Morgantown, West
Virginia, for my dad's work. And, *argh!* I hated roll call. Remember
that in grammar school? You probably don't. Because your name is
normal. My first day in each grade always began like this:

"Suzie Kalfer . . ."
"Mike Kauffman . . ."
No . . . Lord . . . no . . .
"Chris Kennedy . . ."
Oh . . . we're just one away . . .

Second grade photo

"Hmm. Uh . . . is this . . . okay, we've got, uh . . . How do you say your name?"

And all the heads would snap around to check out the weird kid. I wanted to disappear.

Just skip me! Please skip me!

I remember being encouraged by the teacher to use my "playground voice" because I would always whisper; I was so embarrassed. When you have a weird name and your hair and skin are different and you don't blend in, it's a long year. You have to work extra hard to make friends. And just when you do, it's time for the next grade and a new roll call. Gulp. My saving grace came once a year when the class would tackle world geography and everyone chose a region to study. I always picked my ace in the hole, a country in the Middle East. Lebanon—*yes!* That's for me. My mom would bake baklava, we'd play authentic Arabic music, and my parents would actually come in to class to answer questions. They told stories about the Great Sphinx and other wonders from our faraway land. They were rock stars. And for once, so was I!

By fourth grade, Hala, Adel, and I had made a solid set of friends, living in West Virginia on a typical suburban street with the Renns, Rentons, Cignettis, and Khourys.

We were then informed that we were moving. To Nigeria.

What?!

My dad had a job opportunity that would take us first to Egypt for six months, then on to Nigeria. Looking back, I respect my parents' approach: This is what we're doing. It's not going to kill you. See the world. Get on board. But back then it was challenging.

Here's how my first day of fifth grade unfolded in Nigeria:

"*Oooga waga . . . Oooga waga . . .*" That's what my ten-year-old ears heard anyway.

The class was having a tribal language lesson. All the boys had three tribal scars raked into their faces and the girls had their hair wrapped in thin wire that was then bent backward.

I thought, *Where have I landed?!*

Adel was just one grade below me, so he and I were in the same school—the one with all Nigerian kids and tough teachers. Adel had a particularly cranky instructor, so I would listen with all my might in case he cried out.

In my classroom, the teacher always wiped the chalkboard with his hand, so his palm was perpetually white with chalk dust. One day, a little boy raised his hand to ask a question. I was encouraged— *Okay, kids here ask questions, too. Great!* The little boy asked, "Why does the word 'business' look like it should be pronounced *bus*-ness?"

Big mistake. My teacher grabbed the kid's T-shirt and whacked him with that white hand, puffs of chalk dust wafting with every whack. I was in shock. The teacher yelled, "Don't say what you don't understand!" Whack!

Wow. Adel and I would run home and say, "You can't believe it! They're hitting kids!"

But my parents would hear none of it. They'd tell us to hush. "Oh, stop being such a baby," my mom would say. "You're spoiled!" They were dismissive of our whining. After all, the Nigerian kids were well behaved and super smart. And you know what? That little stint abroad once again shrunk the world for us. Becka Ray and Alaywa Lee from weird Nigeria became just classmates to us. We didn't even see the tribal scars after a while. We learned that not everybody looks and sounds the same. And now that the chalk dust has settled, I think that's a terrific lesson for kids.

For sixth grade, we moved back to the United States, first to West Virginia briefly, and then to Alexandria, Virginia. Our street was like the United Nations. The neighbors across the street were Greek, next

Summer in Egypt: Me, my mom, brother, grandfather, and sister, 1968

door Chinese. The Kotbs simply represented one more set of coordinates on the world map. Still, this was a hard transition for me. Eleven was an awkward age in the looks department (Who okayed those stop-sign glasses, Mom?!). At least we had a cool house. For the first time, we kids each had our own room. We'd never before seen a laundry chute and loved having a basement. We eventually got settled into our new school and looked forward to summer. That's when our family traveled to Egypt. And that's why, if you rummaged through the building blocks of our young lives, you'd find some pyramids. Once a year, we'd travel thousands of miles to visit relatives. (Y'know that "Over the river and through the woods" routine? Well, for me, that river was the Nile.) We'd stay with my mom's parents in Heliopolis, a suburb of Cairo. My cousins lived close by and so did my dad's relatives, who all lived in the same family-owned building. I got a kick out of figuring out which balcony belonged to which family member. There, we were clearly the American kids, bopping around with our backpacks and high-top sneakers. My relatives could *not* believe we didn't speak Arabic.

"Haram!" they'd gasp. "How is this? *Harammmm!"*

Haram has two meanings. One is sweet, like when you might say, "Oh, my goodness!" out of concern for a child who's taken a tumble. The other is rooted in alarm—like when you're worried for a soul.

"Harammmm!" they'd say.

There it was, the alarm. Something about "being against God" or "burning in the fiery depths of hell." My response was to recite, out loud, the one Arabic prayer my parents taught us. For the most part, though, Egypt was a blast. Imagine, as a kid, having the exotic pyramids as your playground. We used to put our hands on the massive stones and imagine how old they were. We (scared to death and crying) rode camels and donkeys and played in our infinity sandbox. Since

Hala and me, playing at the pyramids, 1981

our parents brought us to Egypt regularly, the world seemed small. We hopped on a plane and were across the globe. Sampling a different culture wasn't the chance of a lifetime, it was just summertime.

Back in the states, my dark eyes, skin, and hair weren't ever going to change or assimilate. They have always created, and probably always will, a cultural conundrum now and then. As a result, I sometimes offend people by accidentally betraying "our" ethnic group. One that I didn't even realize I was in—huh?

My all-white basketball team in high school played an all-black team twice a season. I was No. 24. At the end of the game, every player walked through opposing lines to shake hands. But no one on the other team would shake mine. I didn't get it. What was going on? Some of the black players said, "Oh, really? You're with *them*?" I had accidentally betrayed them. To this day, I'll sometimes get the "Which team are you on?" confusion. One afternoon, riding the subway in New York City, I was standing next to a black guy, and a white guy came on board shaking a can. Passengers were digging into their pockets for change and the black guy next to me said, "Yeah, do you think if that was 'us' (there it is), they'd be givin' 'us' any money?" I dunno. I just wanted to play basketball and get to my subway stop.

One of the biggest challenges of looking different is dating. In junior high, I remember being just fine with the two-dimensional male. I tacked a poster on the back of my bedroom door featuring hunky Erik Estrada from the television hit *CHiPs*. (I loved Barry Manilow, too.) But I had no confidence with living, breathing boys. One time in seventh grade, I was playing Spin the Bottle in a friend's basement. The bottle landed on Todd Oakes, who I thought was *so* hot! But he wouldn't kiss me. Hot Todd said, "Look, I think this is going too far." I was crushed and confused. Too far, like too intimate? Or, too far, as in thousands of miles away to Egypt too far? He may as well have broken that bottle over my head.

I just had no confidence with boys. And no experience, either. My parents—curses!—decided to go Old World with that segment of our upbringing. Dating? No way. In Egypt, marriages weren't arranged, but they were certainly well researched. My parents weren't comfortable with the American "girl-meets-boy-meets-four-more-boys" routine. Even if we *did* go out, you may as well have turned the car around the minute it left the driveway. Our curfews were ridiculously tight. The Kotbs were always the first to have to leave any place. Crimes common in the United States (like kidnapping and random shootings) were un-heard of in Egypt and made my mom and dad *very* nervous. If my dad answered the phone and heard a boy's voice on the other end, he'd snap, "No calling here!" Click. My parents' plan was to find a nice family with a kid they could "research." Sounds smart to me now, but then? Cruel!

Occasionally, I took matters of the heart into my own hands. Like in junior high, when I made out with Jon Zachman in our basement while my parents were at work. Or so I thought. We were interrupted by the sound upstairs of the front door opening. Yikes! Downstairs, I saw one Jon Zachman spinning out the back door like a whirling dervish. Close one!

The first formal high school dance I went to was not like yours, with the cozy photos in the living room and the special dress. My parents would hear nothing of me going to a dance, so arrangements for my junior prom were undercover. Someone sneaked me a dress, I lied about being with someone else, and I met up with my date, John Langanke, at someone's house. And that would be the house of the Slurpee. Yep. We rendezvoused at 7-Eleven and snapped our photos right there in front of the building. Norman Rockwell and my parents would *not* have approved, but John and I had a ball.

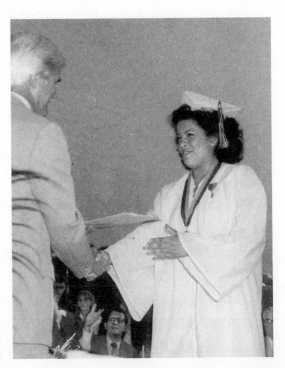

Fort Hunt High School
graduation, 1982

I'd find out in later years that dating in Egypt—where I looked the part—was just as challenging. When I visited Cairo the summer after college, my relatives tried to set me up with a nice Middle Eastern boy. (Not that I'd asked.) I'm surprised they even felt I'd "work" over there, based on my lackluster performance at a family gathering when I first arrived. I was sitting in my grandmother's living room with a large group of relatives—cousins, aunts, and uncles on each side of me. My legs were crossed, one at a sharp right angle, foot resting on the other, heel pointing out. I noticed the people to my left grew quiet. Hmm. After a few minutes, I recrossed my legs the same way in the opposite direction. The people to my right became hushed. What was going on? Finally, one of my relatives shouted, "Eee! Look at what you are doing! Pointing the bottom of the foot at the people! And then to the other!"

You'd think I'd pointed a gun!

But to Egyptians, that heel bottom is like double flipping the bird. I was basically double flipping off relatives to the left and then rotating the birds to the other side of the family. Nice touch, Hoda.

Still, my relatives thought they needed to set me up. During my visit, I'd be sitting on the couch and there'd come a knock-knock at the door.

"Hoda, someone's at the door for yooooouuuu . . ."

Oh, Lord.

"This is Mohammed. He's from Cairo. He's studying engineering . . . and he has a Mercedes."

Really? He also has on a long white man dress.

Okay, call it a dishdash.

Still, am I supposed to be turned on by that?

A river of respectable guys with good educations and backgrounds flowed through the door, but I wanted nothing to do with any of them. Even if Prince Charming himself had walked in, he was not the cool, progressive guy I wanted. Plus, never tell me what to do. Bad approach. Worse than the man dress.

So, there you have it. I struggled for years to fit in as a kid. Hardly a rare tale—it would probably be a chapter in everyone's book about their life. It's easy for me now at forty-six. New York City is a melting pot, plus I've ditched the stop-sign glasses for contacts. I will always be asked "What is you?" And while I'll proudly explain I'm Egyptian . . . again, the answer in my head will always be: *I'm just me.*

2

MY FAMILY

I have pictures of my family everywhere. In my apartment, stacks of photos sit on each table and shelf. My refrigerator door looks like a bulletin board. In my office at work, frames of all shapes and sizes are filled with photos of my mom, Hala, Adel, and me. Always huge smiles.

I don't have many frames that include photos of my dad. Odd, but I guess it's too painful to look into the eyes of someone who's not a phone call away.

My Dad

When I was a junior in college, my dad died. To write those words is still such a shock, even after twenty-four years. Like most girls growing up, I put my dad on a pedestal. Each year I built the platform a little higher. As the middle child, I had the prized firstborn on one side

With my dad and Hala in Morgantown, West Virginia, 1974

and the coveted only son on the other. That left me always eager to win my dad's approval; and he was one tough cookie. He was old school and intimidating to me. He was very accomplished and very busy at his job, and he kept the bar of expectations raised high for his kids. I remember one day in grade school I brought home a C– in math, and it nearly broke me. I couldn't muster up the nerve to go downstairs and show my dad the report card. "Just go tell him," my mom insisted.

I slunk down the stairs, handed him the poison paper, and turned my back, hugging my sides. "Why did you get this grade?" he asked. I turned back around and came up with some mumbo jumbo. I cringed. He simply said, "Go upstairs and study some more."

So much of my emotion for my dad stayed tucked inside my heart and my head.

One rare night when it was just he and I sitting at the kitchen table, he asked me a harmless question: "What's on your mind?" *What?!* His question took me off guard—struck me as so unexpectedly personal. In a display of complete emotional insanity, I shot up from the table and exploded into tears. There was so much bottled up inside me that the cap just blew. I was simply out of practice with that tone of conversation with my dad. Emotions were just not something he and I shared. The one and only time I saw my dad cry was when his mom died. I had stepped into my parents' bedroom and caught him sitting on the edge of his bed with his face in his hands. He didn't hear me enter, so I slipped out, my stomach in knots. Seeing my dad vulnerable was extraordinarily unsettling to me. I just never thought of him as someone's son. I felt a jarring mix of sadness for him and fear for me—my dad was human, not superhuman.

Because he'd achieved so much in his life through hard work, my dad wanted us to follow the same path and reap the rewards of living in a free and limitless country. Learning, to him, was the key to everything. Even our dinner table was a classroom. "How do you say 'fork' in Arabic?" he'd ask through bites of supper. There was always chicken, rice, vegetables, and current events. "What is going on overseas right now?" he'd ask. "What are you reading?"

Around the time I was a junior at Virginia Tech, my dad was working harder than ever. He had just left his government job to start his own business: International Petroleum Consulting Service. *How perfect*, I thought. My dad was the president of his business, with an office on Pennsylvania Avenue, right down the way from the other president. (I told you, the pedestal was always growing.) Hala was already out of college, but Adel and I were still students at Tech. He was a sophomore and a proud member of the TKE fraternity. He always joked that he planned to crash one of my Tri Delt sorority formal dances.

And one night he did. I was all dressed up, but Adel walked in wearing street clothes. What was going on?

Adel and me in
Puerto Rico, 2010

He pulled me aside and told me to come outside. I was getting scared and I refused to leave.

"No. Tell me now. What's going on?"

"Dad had a heart attack."

"Is he okay?" *Please say yes, Adel.*

"No."

My parents were at the gym when it happened. Exercise was a big part of our family life. We rode bikes together, my parents played tennis on weekends, and we all had a membership at the local spa. My dad always waited outside the spa workout room for my mom to come out, but on this day, he wasn't there when she was finished.

Curious, she asked a spa worker to please call out his name in the men's locker room. The worker came back out to tell her that no one had responded. She figured he'd had a hard time pronouncing Abdel Kotb and assumed my dad was simply delayed. Then, she saw medics running down the hall and into the men's gym. That's when she began to panic. "What color is the shirt of the person you're helping?" she frantically asked a medic. He ran into the gym without answering, but on his way back out for more supplies told her "blue." My mom's heart sank. Her world shattered. The same spa worker came out of the gym holding my dad's wallet. He gave it to my mom. How could this be? My fifty-one-year-old father had just undergone a physical and was told he had the heart of a thirty-year-old.

When that no came out of Adel's mouth, I began screaming. My Tri Delt sisters tried to hug and comfort me, but I wanted none of it. I pushed them away and ran outside. Adel's friend dropped us off at his dorm and we just sat in my brother's room. We played the James Taylor *Greatest Hits* album for what seemed like the whole night. I must have picked up the needle and plopped it back down a thousand times. We flew home the next day to a house full of people and to what is now simply a blur in my mind. The only image I can remember is my mother. She was a complete mess in her bedroom, saying over and over through tears, "When the husband dies, the wife goes shortly after." We were terrified we'd lose her, too. In my fear, I wrote my mom a letter that night:

> I love you. I love you more than I love anyone on the face of this earth. You're the one who makes me smile, the one who brightens my day. You're my inspiration and your inspiration is a wonderful man who gave to you and all of us unselfishly. I watched how Dad could brighten your day with just a few kind words. He gave you strength and gave the same to us. Dad gave so much of himself and will always live. Do you understand? Just because he's not physically here doesn't mean he's not here. I carry a part of Dad wherever I go. You must know that all Dad gave to you can never die.

I'm struck now by the desperation in that letter. It was my attempt at a life preserver for my mom. I was petrified I'd lost both my parents.

For quite a while, I lived in a daze. Back at school, I refused to wear my contact lenses or my glasses (and I'm basically legally blind). I silenced my world with a steady stream of music playing in both ears. I walked around like a zombie. It was just easier. In class, nothing mattered. In the middle of a test one day, I just checked out. I started packing up my backpack, and the professor said, "You can't leave. If you don't pass this test, it's going to hurt your average." I didn't care. I didn't say one word. I started to walk out with all my stuff, and out of the corner of one blind eye, I saw my friend, Peggy, get up. She left her test behind, picked up her bag, and followed me out of the classroom. I walked straight to the duck pond, where it was quiet and soothing. I plopped down on a picnic table and Peggy sat down next to me. She didn't say one word. We just sat. You can probably name people like that in your life, too—someone who, at one of the worst moments in your life, sacrificed their own time, their own tears, just for you. Those are the angels in our lives.

Peggy and I graduate
from Virginia Tech, 1986

About ten years ago, Adel found a letter in my dad's desk that we'd never seen before. It was from the bigwigs at West Virginia University, where he was chairman of the Department of Mining Engineering. Apparently, he had written to them and made his case for a promotion. He wrote that while he had a doctorate, some of the other professors did not; yet he was still the lowest-paid on staff. They wrote back with a "Sorry, Dr. Kotb . . ." That's when we moved to Alexandria, Virginia.

I have so much respect for my father. He never let his kids know there were things that held him back in life. He simply pushed forward, and pushed us, too. I know to this day he still pushes me, motivates me. And I crave the thing I can't have. I want him to see that I grew into a person he'd be proud of. I crave hearing him say, "You did it. You're there." Thanks, Dad. You're one of the true angels in my life.

My dad, 1957

Hala and Adel

Picture this: my arm getting slammed in the door over and over and over again. On purpose—by my sister. I guess I *should* mention it's because I have a huge handful of her hair clenched in my claw—and I won't let go.

That is a snapshot of my young life with my sister. And with my brother, too.

Remember how I told you I used to listen for Adel's scream when we went to school in Nigeria? That's because I knew the sound of it well. I caused it so often. He and I would wrestle every morning as kids. "I'll meet you downstairs!" we'd say. Our games were not for the faint of heart or head. Adel has a scar on his right eyebrow from me pushing him into a bookcase—for fun.

We three grew up thick as thieves. Thieves who stole stuff from each other. We fought hard and played hard, but if any outsider tried to mess with one of us—watch out. One year, Adel was stinking it up in school. (Turns out, he just needed glasses.) He brought home a D in math from a teacher I'd had the year before. He just was not seeing, and therefore not completing, his homework that quarter. When he stepped it up a notch (with glasses) and did all the assignments the next quarter, he *still* got a D. What was up with that? I got out the phone book with Adel sitting next to me and looked up the teacher's home phone. (Good plan, Hoda.)

"Hello, is this Mrs. Tarlano?"

"Uh . . . yes."

"Mrs. Tarlano, this is Hoda Kotb. I'm Adel's sister and I had you last year?"

"Uh . . . yes?" (Read: Are you really calling me at *home*?)

I went on to explain the inconsistency of effort in the math homework proportional to the ultimate grade given, blah, blah, blah . . . get
it, Mrs. Tarlano? She sort of did. She upgraded Adel to a C-. We sibs
protected each other. If you watch our home movies, the dynamic
hasn't changed much on who wears the pants in our trio.

Hala.

She wears 'em. I iron 'em, and Adel makes sure we're clear about it.

From one winter in Morgantown, West Virginia, there is grainy film
of Hala lounging on a snow sled. I launch her down the hill, then pull up
the sled for her *every* time. To *this* day, I just shake my head as we walk to
the beach—Hala in front sans anything, me trying to keep up, weighed
down like a rented mule with all the day's gear. So it goes. My sister and
brother are constants in my life. "Irwin" was (and still is) our joint nick-
name, plucked from a cartoon we saw as kids. Okay, it's weird. But that's
how it is. On Christmas presents to each other, the tags all read "Irwin"
and we just figure out through the handwriting who gets what.

Hala and me, 2009

• • •

Hala is one of the reasons we've all stayed so close through the years. She is the glue. Her commitment to family is old school, rooted in the theory that years and miles don't stand a chance against the bond of blood. She's fiercely protective, loyal, and at the ready. When my dad died, Hala moved in with my mom. She also lived with my brother at one point when she moved back from working overseas in London. She stayed with me for about five months when I needed help and support with a health issue. Whenever our family ties have loosened—for college, careers, or day-to-day life, Hala has been there to tighten the loop. Many years ago, she engineered a tradition of weekly Sunday dinner together. Glue. With a side of chicken and rice. Hala now lives overseas again, and here's the weird part: somehow, this girl will know on an average Wednesday what I had for breakfast, that Adel's in a bad mood, and that my mom has the sniffles. And she's in Dubai, eight hours ahead of us all! "Call Mom, she just got new shoes," she'll inform me from nearly 7,000 miles away. "She's going to that thing tonight, so ask her about that, too." Hala is Command Central. And my brother is Steady Central. Adel is patient, reliable, humble, funny, and as generous as they come. When I got my first job out of college in Mississippi, I was flat broke. And I needed a car. Adel had worked all summer at a Church's Chicken, pocketing a total of $1,000. He saved every dime. The car dealer was demanding that I put money down, but I didn't have a penny. Adel gave me his entire summer salary to buy that car. Without hesitation, he wrote me a check. He never said one word about it, either—there's none of that with him. He's gold. And now, he has a little gold nugget named Hannah. I promise I won't go on and on like a typical aunt, but it must be said: Hannah is pretty much the perfect niece. She certainly came into our lives at a perfect time, when life seemed to need a few more watts. On May 29, 2007, Hannah lit up the delivery room and hasn't stopped since. She's subtracted years from my mom's life and added a million smiles to all of ours. When she was first beginning to reveal her personality, I'd think, *Okay, okay,* when my mom would tell me about little Hannah's brilliance.

"Did you see what Hannah *drew*?!" exclaimed Teta ("Grandma" in Arabic).

"Yeah, Mom . . . I think it's a line. But, yes. It's good."

And then, the more I got to know her, as I was able to travel more often to see her, I jumped right on board the "Crazy for Hannah" train. Toot! Toot! I'll marvel to friends, "Hannah said, 'It's kinda windy' when we were at the beach! Who says 'kinda windy' at her age?! This kid's a *genius*!" Hannah changes the room. She's instant happiness. She makes you relook at the small things and see the big, huge importance of them. Brown ringlets bobbing, she loves to scour my apartment for

Hannah and Aunt Hoda, 2009

anything to throw out—just so we can go to the *very cool* trash chute. How did I miss that? It *is* very cool. We Kotbs had no idea a part of the family puzzle was missing until that sweet little pink piece snapped into place. Now we feel incomplete when Hannah's not around.

"Is Hannah going with us?"

(Pause.) "Oh, okay. I don't wanna go either . . . not gonna be any good."

Adel takes on the role of daddy with ease. After all, he's had the stuff you need in a Parent Tool Box since he was a kid—huge heart, infinite patience, even keel, protective. His wife, Colleen, completes

Adel, Colleen, and Hannah

the set as a really great mom and wife. She and Adel met each other on Match.com, two diamonds in the rough world of Internet dating. Physically, they are polar opposites: the fair-skinned, redheaded Irish lass and the dark-skinned, dark-haired Egyptian. But their hearts are identical—in love with the other's. I watch them raise Hannah and marvel at the safe place they've created for her. Boy, that kid. My brother and sister. I am one lucky Irwin.

My Mom

Every morning, immediately after I get off the air, I call my mom in Washington, D.C., for her requested rundown of how the fourth hour unfolded.

"Eye-eye," I say.

"Eye-eye, Hodie." she answers.

We then dig into a mile-high pile of minutia that only a mother could amass, question after question. "What dress did you wear? What color was it? Did you have fun? Were you warm enough?" Like I'm a kid who's come home from a day at school. She hasn't seen the show yet because she's working, but a video awaits at home. "We had on so-and-so from the new TV series such-and-such and she was really great, Mom. It tasted really awesome, Mom. I wore the red dress with the black shiny heels, Mom." No greater cheerleader could exist for a daughter. (At least not this one.) But Lord help her neighbors.

My mother has, in a massive videotape library in her apartment, every story I've ever covered, every show I've ever appeared on. And I assure you, quality is *not* required to make it into that library.

"Did you see the *Dateline NBC*—the murder mystery? How about *Your Total Health*? No . . . last time you did not see *this* one . . . sit down." She's relentless.

And now, she has TiVo. To her neighbors, I'll just say this: I am *so* sorry.

My mom also thinks she's solely responsible for the *Today* show ratings in D.C. "Wow, Mom—our hour got a 3 rating in D.C. today!" I'll tell her. "I know—I sent emails to Linda and Nancy, and I also sent out an eblast to friends to watch," she'll calculate. "I'm not surprised."

My mom is a kick. I get that I have no perspective since she's my mom, but you'd be hard-pressed to find anyone with a more positive outlook on life or who shows more joy in living it. "Guess what?!" she'll say to me. "I am going to a Conway Twitty concert!" She's already bought the skirt, the boots, and the hat. She'll call and say, "You are *not* going to believe it! Umi and I got tickets to go see Tina Turner!" My mom loves nothing more than a new experience, with or without

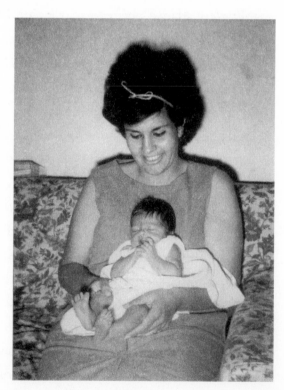

Mom: My inspiration
from Day One

someone to share the journey. She gathers friends as she goes. When she vacationed in Paris and England by herself, she came back with a purse full of names and phone numbers of people she'd met. The same thing happens on the train, a café—wherever there are people. She is open to everyone and everything. Life is exciting to my mom.

And she's incredibly strong. Always has been. During one of our vacations to Egypt in October of 1973, she was put to the test—with three small children. The Arab-Israeli conflict exploded while we were on vacation there. My dad was not with us because he was in Ibadan, Nigeria, readying the house we'd move into in the coming year. So my mom was on her own with three kids when the fighting came to a head. While we slept at my grandmother's house, word came that all U.S. citizens were to leave Egypt. *Now.* My mom woke us and herded us into the living room. Officials had arrived carrying two different stamps, one red and one blue. Hala, Adel, and I held out our hands for the red stamp, signifying U.S. citizenship. My mom got hers and we headed out into the black night. Cairo was completely dark because the streetlights and car headlamps were painted blue to "hide" the city from bombing raids. My mom wrangled us onto a bus headed for Bengazi, Libya. Leaving by air was not an option. The Cairo airport had been closed down. Once in Libya, we were to board an airplane and fly to Italy.

There were about six buses in our caravan. (I don't recall this, but fellow evacuee accounts describe a green cross painted on the roof of each bus.) It was now around three o'clock in the morning and we kids thought this was a fine adventure. There was whispering and huddling and being awake at an odd hour. Someone aboard the bus handed out food rations to last the several-day ride to Bengazi. Adel and I proceeded to polish off the entire stash! Such American kids. "What have you done?!" cried my poor mom. We then whined and complained about the roadside bathrooms: "But there's only a grate, Mom—and *no* toilet paper, only newspapers." She told us, "Just go!"

Our journey would cover about 700 miles, but before we reached Bengazi, we had to get across the Libyan border. Evacuee accounts of the crossing depict utter chaos. Countless cars, trucks, and buses were all trying to exit Egypt into Libya. The Libyan government refused to let people through unless their passports were translated into Arabic. I remember my frantic mom filling out everyone's forms because she was the only American on our bus who understood Arabic. On the last leg of the trip, a terrible sandstorm made driving nearly impossible. After a few hours, we finally arrived in Bengazi. A U.S. representative arranged for hotel rooms, and the next morning we boarded a Bulgarian airplane for Rome. It was pouring rain when we landed. My mom somehow dragged three kids through the dismal night, not knowing a lick of Italian, terrified for her husband left behind in Nigeria.

Family dinner in Florida, summer 2007

• • •

To this day, my mom's unsinkable spirit is an inspiration to me. For nearly thirty years, she's worked at the Library of Congress. Everyone knows Sameha simply as "Sami." Along with 500 miles of shelved books, her closest friendships are cataloged in that library. They are as much the value of work to my mom as is the work itself. She and her longtime buddies plan fun coffee breaks, wear costumes to the office on Halloween, and often get together outside work. I can't remember a time when my mom didn't work. She has forever been on the move: a go-getter. When Adel and I had a paper route as kids, my mom would get up *before* us at the crack of dawn to drop off the *Washington Post* at different corners. That would lighten our load as we walked and delivered papers to each area. Her morning ritual was to run before work. Even when it was snowing, she would try to wake us up to join her. We wanted nothing to do with it! No surprise, then, at sixty years old, she vowed to run the Marine Corps Marathon. Hala, Adel, and I joined her in D.C. to cheer her on. We waved to her at the starting line and mapped out all the spots where we'd be able to yell to her. At Mile 3 she looked great, waving and smiling. Mile 6 was a problem. Temperatures had soared and the heat was getting to my mom—with 20 miles to go! When we saw her again at Mile 10, she was really struggling.

"Someone has got to get in there with her!" said Hala. "She needs support!"

Adel was wearing loafers, Hala had on sandals, and I had on sneakers—of course.

"Get *in* there!" Hala told me. "Mom needs you!"

For the next few miles, I ran with my mom. We talked and walked and ran when we could. *Just move forward. Just move forward.* I knew there was a time cutoff for when she had to reach a certain landmark, in this case, a bridge. In just a few minutes, officials were going to open the bridge back up to traffic. All runners who did not get there in time would have to board a bus. Horrors! Just four miles from the finish line and she'd be riding in a bus? No way. As the police officer was whistling us toward the bus, I grabbed my mom and we started running, traffic licking at our heels. We were crazy with fatigue but determined to do this! Somehow, we kept going. Eventually, we heard the trumpeting of the Marine Corps Band welcoming runners to the finish line. I stopped short so my mom could cross by herself.

She did it!

I was crying, she was crying, my sister was crying, and my brother, too. (Although to this day, he claims he was just hungry.)

"I was *not crying* . . . I was just hungry, *okay*?" Adel insists every time we tell the story.

(By the way, Adel did the same for me when I ran the Boston Marathon in 1996. He was my wingman the last six miles, wearing jeans and, yep, loafers.)

With marathon mom

P.S.

People often ask me about my mom's baklava recipe that I reference from time to time on the *Today* show. Baklava is a sweet pastry made with layers of phyllo dough, filled with chopped nuts, and sweetened with honey. My mom learned to make it with her family in Egypt and turned out endless batches for us kids while we were growing up. She still does. She either mails it or hands it off to me at the end of a visit.

"Don't you eat that on the train!" she warns. That's because she wants me to take it to work and share it with the crew. She gets the biggest kick out of how long it takes for a pan of her baklava to disappear on set.

"Six minutes, Mom. It was gone in six."

"Reeeeeeallly." She smiles. She knows the baklava is her thing.

"Did everyone like it? Did Matt get a piece?"

"Yes, Mom. I cut Matt a piece."

Prepare to cut yourself a piece, too! My mom said I could share her recipe with you. Get ready. It is *heaven*.

SAMI'S BAKLAVA

SYRUP

 ½ cup sugar

 ½ cup honey

 1 cup water

 1 teaspoon vanilla extract

FILLING

 6 cups of walnuts, ground into small pieces (but not *too* fine)

 1 cup sugar

 2 tablespoons butter

 2 tablespoons water, or more as needed

INGREDIENTS

 1 16-ounce package of phyllo dough (I use Athens Fillo [Phyllo]
   Dough, with forty 9 × 14-inch sheets)

 4 sticks of unsalted butter

DIRECTIONS

1. Make the syrup by heating all the ingredients together in a saucepan until the sugar melts. Then put it in the refrigerator to cool.

2. Make the filling by mixing the walnuts and the sugar, then adding
   the butter and 2 tablespoons water, plus more as needed. (Filling
   should be just moist.)

3. Melt 4 sticks of unsalted butter.

4. Unfold packages of phyllo dough sheets.

5. Brush 9 x 13-inch pan with butter; take 3 to 4 sheets of phyllo dough at a time, put in the pan, and brush with butter (keep the remaining dough covered with a piece of foil to prevent from drying out).

6. After you've brushed approximately 12 sheets with butter, spread on half of the walnut filling and continue adding more phyllo dough sheets. Spread on the remaining walnut filling. (Make sure to leave enough sheets to cover the last walnut filling, and to brush every 3 to 4 sheets with butter. Drizzle any remaining butter on the top.)

7. Cut entire pan into diamond shapes. (Don't cut all the way through.)

8. Bake in preheated 325°F oven for 1 hour or until golden brown. (After baking, you may decide to put the pan under the broiler with the oven door opened for a few minutes for a more golden color on top. But watch out! It burns easily.)

9. Add cooled syrup and complete the diamond shape cutting all the way through. Remove from pan immediately. Serve and enjoy!

Reminder: Keep the phyllo dough covered with foil while working with it—it prevents the dough from drying out.

My Hair

Bad hair in 1987 . . .

Bad hair in 1996 . . .

Bad hair with BB King!

Okay, why is my hair in the family section? Because, really . . . my hair is like a family member.

It's the misbehaving brown-headed stepchild that everyone is always taking about, worrying about, catering to, and threatening to "cut off" if she doesn't start behaving. My hair even has its own room, otherwise known as my bathroom cabinet. It's decorated with aluminum spray cans, plastic squirt bottles, and posters that scream, "No-Worries Hair!" and "Miracle Mend!" It smells like kiwi, aerosol, and mud. Honestly, if you studied a pie chart of my spending and looked for all the dollars I've dropped on "product," there would be no slices, just full-on pie.

But really, can you put a price on hope? Straightening, relaxing, smoothing, conditioning, cleansing, highlighting, lowlighting *and* . . . the all-important (angels sing) "blowout." I farm out for the blowout. Thirty or forty dollars per? Priceless. Worth every cent.

I don't know what you do when relatives come to visit. Go out to lunch? Sit and chat? Thumb through photos of all the special things you've recently done? Not the Kotb women. Oh, no, no. We immediately go and get a blowout. This is the equivalent of Xanax for us. When our hair is right, all is right in the world.

I can tell immediately if a salon is emotionally and physically equipped for the job. If the stylist looks at my hair, gasps under her breath, and grabs for a flat paddle brush, I'm gone. Only the truly skilled know you don't bring down a jungle cat with a dart gun. You use a round brush.

And if you date me, you'd better get on board with the lid. I always know a guy "gets" me when he's as panicked as I am at the first sniff of humidity or splat of a raindrop.

"I see it, I see it! I've got it!" he scrambles. "I've *got* the umbrella!"

For my thirty-seventh birthday, a sweet guy from work asked me out on a date. I bought a new outfit and, of course, got my hair blown out.

He said, "I've got something very special planned . . ."

How wonderful!

"And I think you'll love it," he added. "It's an Off-Broadway show."

I love Off-Broadway!

He didn't get me.

When we arrived, the room was like a mosh pit. Everyone was standing up and there was no orchestra. A guy on stage started spraying *water* everywhere! By now, you can guess that for me this is what hell looks like. I became the Wicked Witch of the West, cowering from the deadly water.

What fun for everyone! Except for me and a black girl who ran with me behind the stairs. We looked at each other in horror.

"Who would bring me here?" I gasped. "And on my *birthday*!"

"It's your *birthday*?" she gasped back. "How cruel!"

Water balloons were dropping like bombs. I was in a war zone, not on a date.

Now, I'm hardly high maintenance or vain, but when it comes to this mop—you can't stop it but you have *got* to contain it. Hala, my hair hero, has a detailed list of all the "Kotb-Approved Salons" in cities around the world, as well as their Sunday hours and the day they're closed. She hooks me up.

From the time I was little, my hair was a "thing." Kids used to make fun of my giant frizz and tease (no pun intended) me. "Can I touch it? Can I feel it?" I *so* badly wanted "normal" hair that would swing Farrah-fully when I shook my head. One year, my mom bought me a tan-colored winter cap made of macramé, sort of like the one J.J. always wore in *Good Times*. I wore that thing out. I wore it all the time; in and out of class. It was the perfect cover. At that point, I don't know which was weirder, the J.J. hat or my real hair.

Flash forward to me at *Dateline NBC* and a producer telling me they're sending me to Uganda.

"We're flying you to Uganda . . . to the bush."

I flinched and got a facial tick.

"Uganda? The bush?" *What?!*

"Yes. Uganda . . . to the bush . . . for a week."

My eyes glazed over. All I could think about was my hair—the bush growing huge in the bush—for a week. I immediately went shopping for those battery cartridge things you shove into flat irons and blow-dryers. I knew we wouldn't have power.

They told me, "Oh, no, no—you can't take those—they're combustible on board . . ."

Well, I had bigger issues than that plane going down, so I packed all my hair gear.

Uganda was *all wrong* for me!

I knew that the story was the point and not my hair. Obviously, I get it. *But I had to plug in my hot rollers somehow!* When we arrived in Uganda-be-kidding-me, the only place with power was a nearby hospital. The photographers had already used the only two available outlets to charge their camera batteries. You *know* I eventually found my way into those plugs. But the photogs clearly did not get me.

Neither did the *Today* show producers who created a segment around me doing a triathlon.

"There's *swimming*, right?" I confirmed in shock. Honestly, I'd rather do "Root Canal Week." I wore *three* bathing caps into that ocean water. My brain was squeeeezed to the max, and when I finally finished the swim and pried off the rubber caps one by one—trouble! Of course there was trouble. You normal-haired people have no idea.

Okay, I do realize this one thing, though. I've now hit the hair jackpot with my current job. I'm totally spoiled. Every morning at the *Today* show, I get my hair blown out by the best. I can work out at the gym *without* worrying about sweating. I laugh at a misty morning. And I worry. I worry that someday this job will go away. And by that I mean Laura will go away. It's losing Laura the hair genius that scares me. Laura is my hair angel. She gets me.

Bless you, Laura. (Call me . . .)

PART TWO

Going Live

3

THE TREK

My heart beats to the tick-tock of a deadline. Procrastinating to me is simply a way to create a time crunch. Like this: After I phone in a takeout food order, I'll stay at work as long as possible, then race home to my apartment to meet up with the delivery guy.

Yes! Made it!

That's why television news is the perfect career for me. I need to know that my work day has a start and a fight to the finish. I'm competitive, persistent, and not afraid to risk being the hero or the goat when airtime hits.

I always knew I wanted to be in the news business. I used to imagine myself working as a foreign correspondent. The groundwork was set early. My family talked current events at home, my dad was always listening to news radio, and we watched *60 Minutes* every Sunday. When I read the morning newspaper, the stories felt like *old* news. I loved the idea of live, in-the-moment reporting. Television news.

That's where I work now. If you know me from watching television, you know me at the mountaintop of my career. You see me in nice dresses and high heels; but actually I've spent most of my work life in hiking boots—climbing, climbing, climbing the mountain. Like a lot of career paths, there are a half-dozen base camps to survive before you actually summit. In my industry, those base camps are small and medium television markets, including at least one random city you've probably never heard of. I've lived in my share and have loved them all. Many of my best friends and favorite adventures would not exist without all the packing and unpacking of gear again and again and again.

Finally, after twelve years of trekking, I've made it to the network, where the air is thin. That's where most of us TV folks want to plant the flag.

I graduated from Virginia Tech in 1986 with a bachelor of arts degree in communications. I felt very good. And very not yet ready to work. Instead, I made it my job to explore Egypt and sample a slice of the great big world. I flew to Cairo and moved in with my dad's brother Mokhles, his wife Iman, and their two kids. It was fun, but after a few weeks, I needed more space, more freedom. I knew there was a building in the city that housed the CBS, NBC, and ABC news bureaus. So I walked in and told anyone who'd listen that I'd just graduated from college with a communications degree. Did they need any help? At first, everyone said no. But after a few days, a call from my uncle's friend, and more begging from me, the CBS bureau chief, Penny Rogg, agreed to let me watch and learn. I began my "job" ripping wire, getting coffee, and getting yelled at. I had to figure out a lot of things on my own. Once in a while, I'd get to head out with a crew. Egypt's president might attend a parade or a foreign dignitary might come through town—that's when I got to ask a list of questions or serve as extra help if something newsy happened.

Several months into my bureau experience, the arms-for-hostages story came to a head. The United States was apparently facilitating the sale of arms to Iran to secure the release of American hostages being held in Lebanon. A source had told CBS News in New York that some of those arms were being transported through the Suez Canal aboard a ship owned by Maersk, a Danish company.

Ring, ring!

I was basically by myself in the bureau when a panicked CBS producer called from the States. Our bureau chief, Penny, was back in the United States on business, so I was "on duty" along with a couple of male photographers sitting around reading magazines.

"You need to get a helicopter right now," the producer urged, "and shoot this Danish ship we think is carrying arms through the Suez Canal."

Can I get you some coffee instead?

I said okay, hung up, and began to flail my arms and twirl my hands like a whirlybird, nodding at the two men. My Arabic stunk as badly as their English did. They thought I was nuts. Eventually, I got the point across that we needed to secure a helicopter ASAP. The two just laughed. "Not going to happen," they said in broken English. "Is Friday."

Friday in Egypt is like Sunday in America. Everybody is off. Gulp. I called CBS in New York and broke the news about the "weekend" dilemma.

"Well, you'd better get out there first thing in the morning," instructed the producer, "and get us some video of that ship."

And so we did. Early the next morning, two photographers and I found ourselves lying on the ground as close as we could get to the water. In Egypt, it's illegal to videotape the canal for security reasons, so we were very nervous. I was flipping through a book, making sure I could identify the Danish flag that would be flying on the ship.

"Okay. Red flag . . . big white cross."

We identified the correct Maersk ship and shot for about forty-five seconds. The photographer immediately ejected the tape and handed it to me. "Run to the car right now," he told me, "and throw this *under* the seat." I ran, I threw, I came back. The photographer was already shooting more tape—until there came a tap on his shoulder. Two Egyptian police officers patrolling the canal demanded that we leave. But first, they demanded the tape from the photographer. Apologetic and cooperative, he handed them the tape, which they proceeded to yank out by the yard. It was all I could do not to smile like the Cheshire cat. We had already secured what we needed! I'll never forget what a rush it was that night, watching *our* video air on the *CBS Evening News.* Sure, it was a mere five seconds, a tiny piece of the puzzle, but to me it felt like the start of something good.

After about a year in Egypt, it was time to get serious about finding a job. My stint at CBS fueled the fire, *and* I had a plan. My Master Plan, hot off the press, was this: one single job interview at one television station in Richmond, Virginia. That was it. Signed, sealed, delivered. To prepare for my big interview, I got a fresh blowout. I also bought a brand-new green business suit. I looked ready. Except for one thing. My résumé. Chances are, when you go on an interview, you take along a crisp, paper résumé. Not so with news reporters. In television, our résumé is a videotape. In 1987, it was a bulky, black ¾-inch cassette tape, about the size of a Bible. And Oh, Lord, mine was awful. Twenty minutes of god-awful snippets of fake reporting. Picture me—giant hair—babbling about nothing, trying to look like a foreign correspondent. I shot 98 percent of my résumé tape in

Egypt. No cohesive news stories. Just disjointed crap, floating in the ether, connected to nothing:

- me chatting in front of a pyramid
- me yackity-yacking in front of the Sphinx
- me walking and talking along the Nile
- me shouting a question to the visiting former president Jimmy Carter, and he, completely oblivious

Still, as sad and tragic as this sounds, I was totally proud of that twenty-minute debacle. So, with my crappy résumé tape tucked in my purse, I borrowed my mom's car and drove the hour and a half from my house in Alexandria, Virginia, to the sure-thing TV station in Richmond. When I walked into the WTRV newsroom, I thought, *Oh, yes. My future lies here. I will sit—overrr therrre . . . and I will date—him.*

My life in Richmond was taking shape.

The news director took my résumé tape as we stood together in the edit bay. He popped it into the videocassette machine and watched it for a couple of minutes. He then popped it out and said: "Hoda, you're not ready for Richmond."

Um . . . what?

That reaction had never dawned on me. Not for a second. I was ready to work! I asked him what I could do to improve, and he said that I was just too green, too inexperienced. He thanked me for coming. Buh-bye.

As I was leaving in shock, the news director said, "Hoda, wait a minute. I have a buddy who's hiring in Roanoke, Virginia. He's leaving on a trip tomorrow, but if you catch him tonight, I'll bet he'll see you." I said, "Tell him I'm coming!"

I called my mom and explained that, number one, I *did not* want Richmond, I wanted Roanoke. And, number two, I would need the car for a few more hours. So, off to Roanoke, a three-and-a-half-hour drive.

When I walked in, I looked around the newsroom and thought, *Ohhhhkaayyy—not half bad. I will sit there, and I will date—him. Everything will work out fine.* The news director popped my tape into the machine, played it for a few minutes, and said, "Hoda, you are just not ready for Roanoke."

Who in the *hell* is not ready for Roanoke? (Apparently, me.)

The news director said I was not experienced enough, but with some work, he might want to hire me in a few years. Oh, and—buh-bye.

As I was leaving, he said, "Hoda, wait a minute. I have a buddy who's hiring in Memphis. He's going to be at the conference I'm going to, but I'll bet if you catch him tomorrow morning, he'll hire you." So I said, "Tell him I'm coming."

Tennessee is a long, skinny state and Memphis is at the *other* end. So, I called my mom about the car and started the twelve-hour drive to Memphis. All night long I drove, humming country music and imagining my new life in Tennessee. When I finally rolled into the parking lot of WREG, my hair exploding north in the southern humidity, my green suit looked, well, lived in.

Again, I met the news director. He popped my tape in the machine, watched it, and said (everybody together now), "Hoda, you are just not ready for Memphis. But, best of luck to you." Buh-bye. As I was leaving, he said, "Hoda, before you go, I have a buddy who I think will hire you."

I was in that car driving for ten days. I drove the entire southeastern United States, slept in the car at truck stops, and was turned down three times in Birmingham, Alabama, at all three network affiliates.

Eject tape. Reject me. Rinse. Repeat. (Was it my hair?!)

Dothan, Alabama, turned me down. Does anyone know where Dothan is? I didn't think so. I got rejected in the Florida panhandle a few times, too. All total, twenty-seven news directors told me no. Twenty-seven.

It was clear I had made a mistake and chosen the wrong profession. Maybe that professor in college who told me he didn't think I was one of the few who'd make it in broadcast journalism was right. It was time to give up. Plus, my mom needed her car back. The green suit was tired.

I don't know about you, but when I'm depressed, I listen to sad music. So, I put James Taylor in the tape deck and began driving north aimlessly. I figured I'd drive for a while then look for signs pointing east. Eventually, I'd wind up in Virginia.

Well, a funny thing happened. I got lost. Somewhere in Mississippi. You know how they say God sends us signs? Well, this was a sign—literally. As I was driving, I spotted a billboard that read something like "WXVT: Our Eye is on Your Greenville" (with the CBS eye logo). I thought, *Let me go get rejected there, and then I'll get a map so I can go home and start my career in PR.*

Then I met the man who would change my life.

Stan Sandroni, who just that day had been promoted from sports director to news director, agreed to see me. Stan popped my tape in the machine, and a funny thing happened—he watched it. He watched the whole horrible twenty-seven minutes. My heart pounded. I watched him watch me, and when the tape ended, he hit the stop button. He looked me in the eye and said the words I will never forget: "Hoda, I like what I see."

You do?!

I burst into tears, then burst into the world of journalism.

My first TV job

P.S.

Stan Sandroni was a prince to me when I worked as a reporter at WXVT in Greenville, Mississippi. One day, I was at the station when a panicked Stan came racing into the newsroom.

"Who's got a blazer?!" he asked, short of breath.

"I do," I answered, pointing to a peg on the wall. I figured someone forgot theirs and needed to shoot a stand-up.

"Anne's sick," Stan said to me. "You're anchoring the evening news."

Stop tape. That's so beautiful. That's the beauty of small-market television. The litmus test for who would anchor the evening news was whoever had a blazer!

Well, my heart was pounding, pounding, pounding under that blazer.

Please God, please God, please God—relax! I prayed.

When the red light came on and the floor director cued me, I began to read the teleprompter. It clearly read: "Good evening, I'm Hoda Kotb in for Anne Martin."

I clearly read: "Good morning, I'm Hoda Kotb—"

Stan Sandroni, WXVT news director, 1987

Good morning?!

My brain became obsessed with that "Good morning."

Did I really say "Good morning?" my brain asked, ignoring the job at hand.

Which led to another mess-up.

Now my brain was off the first mistake and latched onto the second. Which led to another and another and another.

The job at hand was way down on my brain's list of priorities. There I was in my blazer, screaming down a hill on a toboggan, no hands.

Whaaaaaaat is haaaaaapppenning?!

When the toboggan finally rammed into the hay bales and the newscast ended, the studio emptied fast. Stan was gone. The crew quickly plucked off my microphone before any more "screw-up cooties" got on it for Anne. I was so depressed. I got out of there and drove directly to the grocery store. I didn't really know anyone in town and I wanted some ice cream. As I walked through the aisles, a woman spotted me and walked over. In a southern accent she said,

"Oh—ma—Gawd. I just saw yeeew," she said, minus a few pearly whites. "I feel sooooo bad for yeeew."

Yeah, well . . . how did my blazer look?

The next day, I went in and apologized to Stan. That beautiful man said he planned to give me another try that night. I did better the second time, and he eventually made me the five o'clock news anchor.

I just wanted you to know that Stan is indeed—the Man.

4

TV NEWS

Plenty of people relocate for work, but when you choose a career in television news, moving is a given. You'd better be ready to pack your bags and leave your friends every few years. The only way to move up is to move out, again and again, until you decide you've "arrived." Sometimes, it's the money, sometimes it's the quality of life, sometimes you're just tired of not having a home base where you can build a life with roots. My work map features pushpins in these markets:

- Greenville, Mississippi (8 months)
- Moline, Illinois (2 years)
- Fort Myers, Florida (2½ years)
- New Orleans, Louisiana (6 years)
- New York City (present)

After years of working in local markets, I arrived at the network, NBC News, in the spring of 1998. The Peacock and the Big Apple were my new what and where—quite a dream team in my eyes. What was the dream team that got me there? Luck and timing.

In early September 1997, I was very happily living in New Orleans and working at the powerhouse station WWL-TV, anchoring the ten o'clock news. That's when Elena Nachmanoff, one of the vice presidents at NBC News, saw some of my work and asked me to fly to New York City for an interview.

Here are two important facts: (1) I happened to be in contract negotiations at the time to re-sign with WWL, and (2) the only job that would ever get me to leave WWL was one at the network.

So, I hopped on a plane to New York wearing what I thought was *so* NYC. Looking back, it was actually an outdated, shoulder-pad-laden suit that was *so* ugly. When I arrived in the city, standing inside 30 Rock made my knees weak. I was incredibly nervous. Over the course of a few hours, the *Dateline NBC* folks took me around to meet everyone, I went through an interview, and then flew home. The experience was surreal and the opportunity was huge. My contract with WWL was ending and the pressure to re-sign was increasing by the day. You can imagine my frustration when an entire week passed after my network interview, with no word.

Finally, Elena called.

"They're not sure you can handle it," she said.

Dateline executives were unsure as to whether I could handle the program's long format style of reporting. In local television, you write stories that *may* last two minutes on tape. *Dateline* stories require at least fifteen minutes, and more often the full hour. Elena said they wanted to fly me back again to do a test. They would give me two crews, a story, and twenty-four hours to put it together. Yikes! Not only was I worried about that, I was still trying to stave off WWL. I knew it was business, but hated having to be secretive. I felt like I was cheating on a boyfriend.

Oh, my God—does he know I went out of town this weekend?!

Once again back in hallowed 30 Rock, I received from *Dateline* a producer, two crews (which I'd never had before), and a stack of papers outlining my story. It was basically a tale of Gotcha versus Gotcha. A Bronx guy named Jimmy Schillaci called Mayor Rudy Giuliani's radio program to complain about what he felt was a red-light sting, run by the police near the Bronx Zoo. He'd not only been issued a ticket while driving by the zoo, Schillaci claimed he had videotaped proof that the police were indeed messing with the red lights. Well, that's when the mayor's office dug up a thirteen-year-old traffic violation and a decades-old rap sheet on Schillaci. Game on.

Dateline set up interviews for me with Schillaci and also with a public advocate from the mayor's office. With what felt like way too many coworkers, I conducted my interviews and shot a standup at the zoo. When we were finished, I went back to the hotel to write the story. I was *freaking* out. The network job of my dreams was on the line and all *my* lines sounded awful—crappy writing, disjointed tale-telling. I was panicking. I paced, I took showers—anything to try to calm down. I eventually went back to 30 Rock to begin looking at my sound bites in the edit bay to complete my story.

That's when Mother Teresa died. Yep. A huge story broke across the world as I was putting together my *very* important tale of traffic lights and who's zoomin' who. Guess who got the red light now? "*Stop* what you're doing. We've got breaking news here," editors told me. "We need these bays."

Dateline told me to fly home. The clock would restart and I could finish my story back in New Orleans. *Yes!* In my pajamas, at my computer, at home, the process was *so* much more relaxed. Conveniently, I could fax *Dateline* my completed script, but I'd have to cut my audio track at WWL and send it. Argh. Once again, I felt like a weasel.

The next step was yet *another* trip back to New York. This third time was to "screen" the story I had written. What a nightmare: me, several senior producers, and *Dateline*'s head honcho, Neal Shapiro, in a dark room, watching and listening to my "long format" story. Silently, they critiqued with pens on paper.

"Okay. Thank you." And then I was flying back to New Orleans.

WWL was all over me about re-signing. What could I do? I had *zero* leverage to get a fast answer from the network. Imagine how ridiculous that would sound:

HODA: "Hey, listen, guys—my station wants to know if I'll re-sign, so can you let me know ASAP?"

NETWORK: "Did Local say something? Did you hear Local say something?"

The network knew there were 18,000 other Hodas in local markets who wanted the job, so no, Local did not say anything. She simply sat in her apartment and waited.

After a few days, I assumed I did not get the gig. I figured I'd re-sign with WWL, which would be a great life. And that's when the phone rang.

"Hoda?" said Elena.

"Yeah."

"This is Elena Nachmanoff."

"Hello."

She said, "You got it."

Pause.

"Put it in a sentence," I smiled. I wanted to remember the moment.

She played along. "You are a correspondent at *Dateline NBC*."

Thankkkk yooooou!!!

I hung up, called my mom, and told her the news. I could hear her yelling to her coworkers in the Library of Congress. (Can you imagine? Yelling in *the* library?)

"My daughter—is a correspondent—for NBC News!" she screamed at the top of her lungs.

I had planted the flag.

If you're wondering what it was like for me to tell WWL I was leaving, it stunk. It really stunk. As with any breakup, things didn't go as well as I'd hoped. The greatest love affairs create the greatest pain when they end. I told my general manager and then my news director. I wished it all felt better, but we all took it hard. Colleagues and residents alike would ask, "How can you leave us?" Ugh. Insert knife and twist. And by that I mean *I'm* holding the knife. How *could* I leave? Some decisions just aren't going to let you get away clean, but it doesn't mean they're wrong.

I agreed to stay through February ratings. My role as a decision-maker in the newsroom faded, and I began to make the break from my home of six years. When I left, the station threw me an unbelievably fun and meaningful going-away party. Today, my relationship with WWL is strong. It will always be the station where I learned the most and that I loved the deepest.

5

THE NETWORK

In April of 1998, I began work at *Dateline*. But before I shot one single inch of videotape, they made me over. And by "they," I mean Lisa Jeer. Lisa is the person NBC calls in to make new hires network ready. She took one look at me, adjusted her sunglasses, and sighed. And sighed again. Everything about Lisa was angular—her hair, her clothes, and her need to perform a 180 on me. She told me we'd start with my wardrobe and then we'd fix—"*that.*" (Her pointer finger was swirling around my general face and hair.) Because "this" and "that" are not my sensitive areas, I was actually *not* offended and vaguely excited. She told me she was coming over to my apartment.

Immediately, she saw trouble.

"No. No. No. No. No," Lisa said, as her two fingers flipped each hanger down the metal rod. She was standing in front of my closet, sorting through what were apparently the most unworthy clothes in the city.

"No. No. No." She stopped at a cowering black blazer. "Maybe with a good tailor." She pulled it out and hung it like squirrel pelt on the closet's panel door.

Lisa sighed again. "We're going to Saks."

When we got to the department store, Lisa was in her element. She was the Chief of the Fashion Police and I was Barney Fife. I trailed behind, catching clothes in her wake as she pulled them off racks and shelves.

"Now go put those pants on," the chief commanded.

Once in the dressing room, I realized Lisa had made a mistake. Good Lord! The pants were skin tight!

"I'm not coming out."

"Get out here."

Squeak, squeak, squeak. The pants and I came hobbling out.

"You're getting those."

"What?!"

"You're getting those pants. You've been wearing clothes that are four sizes too big. You're getting those pants."

Lisa picked out more squeaky pants and fitted blazers, too. Based on what she'd seen in my closet, Lisa did *not* want to take any chances. She snapped photos of each outfit I was to wear, and warned, as if it was a matter of national security, "*Never* stray from these photos."

My God. I actually required a clothing scrapbook. Lisa took pictures of items that mixed and matched and worked together. She even labeled some of the photos:

CASUAL (you're interviewing someone on a farm)

The photo featured a denim shirt, black jeans, black belt with a silver buckle, silver earrings. (Good thing she didn't see my overalls in the closet, right?)

Next, was some sort of a makeup pie chart: *Stay in these color zones, for God's sake!* Again, as if directed at a Navy Seal on a mission.

Then, a trip to the hair salon. Now, you know my hair *is* a sensitive area for me. So, you'd think I would have laid down the law with the chief at this point. But I didn't. Oddly, I just went with the flow, *plus* no one was listening to me anyway.

I met Lisa and Elena at the trendsetting Mark Garrison Salon. The two ladies, Mark, and my hair had a fine time. I was acrylic. No one cared about my insider knowledge of my own hair. The only reason I needed to be there that day was because my hair was attached to my body. Apparently, the big-city folks knew best. And you know what? They really did, from head to toe.

So, from Day One, the network has broadened my knowledge of refining the exterior "package." But, in a more impactful way, working at *Dateline* has also taught me some very important life lessons.

The first is this: Stone Phillips is—so—incredibly—hot. He just is.

The second lesson: Life at the network can be unbelievably glamorous (covering the Olympic Games and the Emmy Awards), *or* it can be extremely *un*glamorous.

6

HOT ZONES

In September 2001, *Dateline* sent me to Pakistan to develop a series called *Why They Hate Us*. It was basically a look into that region's perception of Americans. When we arrived in Pakistan, the first thing we saw was a large, loud protest. Pakistanis were chanting and burning effigies of then-President George Bush. It was perfect footage for our series. We *had* to shoot it. Now, we were an all-female team. Me, the sound girl, the girl producer, the female translator, and our photographer, who was so girlie that he'd be the first to tell you he was one of the gals. So, all us girls began to cover the protest, with everything burning and the chanting heating up.

"*Zaboo! Zaba-zoo!*" yelled the protesters.

Our translator lived in Pakistan but was British. Very well dressed and by-the-book, she immediately began to get agitated.

"This is *quite* haw-stile," she said, huffing and puffing in an English accent.

I agreed but explained, "Yeah, I know . . . but this is what we do."

The chanting crescendoed, *"Zaboo!! Zaba-zoo!!"* The slashing sticks got closer.

Again from the Brit, "This is haw-stile . . . it's naught good . . . we've *gaught* to go!"

I reassured her that this was how we covered the news, and if she'd feel more comfortable in the van, then she should please, go ahead and go.

She stamped her Prada shoe, extremely upset.

"ZABOO! ZABBAZZOOOOOOO!"—even louder and closer now.

Finally, I said to her, "What *are* they chanting?"

Disgusted, she blurted out, "They are chawnting, *"Get these whores out of heah!"*

Hmmm. "Who are the whores?" I asked.

She snarled, *"You! You ah the whores!"*

Oh. Us girls had better get out of here, right? Cheerio, mates. I would learn a lot at *Dateline,* often in hot zones around the globe.

As I've mentioned, my childhood included frequent trips to Egypt, a year in Nigeria, and an overall exposure to cultures across the globe. As a result, my eyes are now kaleidoscopes—they see the many shapes and colors that are the world. That has made my travels for work less intimidating. But not always easy.

When the Iraq War began in March of 2003, I was one of many correspondents asked to head to the Middle East for NBC News. Before we left, the network wanted us to get "schooled" on reporting in a war zone. They flew us to the hills of Virginia for a three-day training camp, where leaders did their best to create situations we might encounter in war.

One challenge began with us getting blindfolded. We were then instructed to walk in a straight line. This skill would come in handy, for instance, in a sandstorm where we'd experience a sand blackout. Boy, did I walk in circles! It was very hard. (Try this at home this weekend.) There was also a building at the camp that was specially rigged with all sorts of booby traps. They told us what clues to look for—strings and pieces of wire. Bombs were set off and we were asked to estimate how far away we thought the explosives were located. And did the bombs release gas or anthrax? Then there was the bag-over-the-head trick. It started with leaders loading us onto a bus. They warned us to be prepared for anything and to stay alert. Suddenly, gunfire broke out and a slew of men came out of nowhere and boarded the bus, screaming. "Put your heads down! Put your heads *down!*" they yelled. (I knew it was fake, but oddly enough, it was still scary.) The men took canvas bags and plunged them down over our heads. The worst part was the tightening of the bag's drawstring around my neck. I've got a bit of claustrophobia, so this was extra disturbing. One by one, they shoved us off the bus. As I said, they told us early on to focus on how things were unfolding—to be aware of our surroundings. But I'll tell you, with my head in a bag, I was distracted and focused only on trying to breathe. And they kept popping me in the back of the head. (*Stop it!*) We were now off the bus with our heads bagged—in the dark. Listening. They began screaming at us again, describing what they were going to do to us and warning us not to move. To keep the male journalists from running, they pulled their pants down around their ankles to serve as leg cuffs. In the meantime, I could hear people (and by that, I mean me) hyperventilating in their sacks. Next, we heard a car door slam, then a vehicle peeling out. One of the reporters asked if everyone was okay. *"Shut up! Shut up!"* Whoops. Some of our "captors" were still there and screaming at us. Afterward, the leaders debriefed us on the facts we'd gathered: How many people were on the scene? What direction did they go? Where were they from?

Mostly I learned this: If I ever get "sacked" again, I should *not* respond the way I did. I tried to suck as much oxygen as I could from within my bag. Bad approach. Instead, I learned I should bite a corner of the bag so I breathe in *fresh* air from the outside, not panic-laden carbon dioxide trapped inside the bag. What a fun fact, eh? You're welcome.

Now, onto the real deal.

Turkey

My network assignment for the Iraq War was to fly to Turkey and cover our troops entering Iraq using the Incirlik Air Base. This is home to the 39th Air Base Wing, located strategically in southern Turkey close to the border of Syria—then Iraq. Here was the sticky wicket: the Turkish government was not convinced it wanted U.S. planes and personnel using its land and airspace to access the war. So, NBC set me up on the roof of an abandoned building to do live shots. The theme was, "Is Turkey going to let us in, or not?"

This went on for weeks. Up to the roof for the live shot.

"Nope, not yet." And back down again.

Up to the roof for the update. "Uh, no." And down.

My mom would call me and say, "Oh, Hodie, I'm so worried about you!"

I appreciated the concern, but—worried?

"About what, Mom?" I wanted to say. "That I'm going to eat bad falafel?"

But instead I told her, "Turn on MSNBC. I'm just *standing* here—on the roof—again."

One day, I was about to do my live roof report when my producer, Roxanne Garcia, approached me. She said in a devastated tone, "We've got some bad news." She was crying. Barely choking out the words, she said, "We lost . . ."

Instantly, I thought, *Oh, my God—it's Kerry Sanders.* He was our reporter who was always in the crossfire. But before I could say Kerry's name, Roxanne said, "David Bloom died." I just stared at her, thinking, *Are you kidding me?* I couldn't process it. Like all of us, I was in shock. I had just seen David on television blazing across the desert in the "Bloom Mobile," an Army tank recovery vehicle retrofitted with satellite and TV equipment. The unit made it possible for him to continuously transmit live rolling reports as U.S. troops made their way toward Baghdad.

I thought, *Who shot David?!*

But it turned out to be a surprise attack from within David's body. At just thirty-nine years old, completely in his element with the 3rd Infantry Division, totally into his battlefield broadcasts from the soldiers' point of view, he died. The killer was deep vein thrombosis and a pulmonary embolism. We were all devastated. I loved David. I kept up with the goings-on of his three daughters, and I've always loved his wife, Melanie. It's still unbelievable.

A few nights later, as we slept in our abandoned building in Turkey, I got a call from one of the guys on the news desk back in New York. He said, "We have a question for you. We want to know if you'll take David's place on that tank going into Baghdad."

Silence. I was so spooked and confused. You like to think you're fearless—and then *that* call comes. Reality calls.

I said, "Let me think about it."

I didn't sleep. I called the people whom I care about and who care about me. As it turned out, there was so much more I valued than sitting in that tank. I just couldn't do it. I felt like I was letting down David. And I felt almost physically sick making that phone call to say, "I just can't do it."

David was more courageous than I am. He is so missed.

Baghdad

In April of 2003, allied troops occupied Baghdad and the war was declared "over." The mammoth bronze statue of Saddam Hussein had been yanked down, but there was still uncertainty as to who was fully in control of the region. That's when we finally found a way into Baghdad. For days, we'd been sleeping on the tarmac of the Kuwait International Airport, hoping for a lift. Finally, there was room for us aboard a C-17 military transport plane. After thirty-plus hours of waiting and flying, we landed at Baghdad International Airport, got off the plane, and wondered, *Now what?* It wasn't like a cab was going to pick us up and take us to Baghdad. So we began to hoof it. We dragged our bags for quite a while, walking toward downtown. We could not get in touch with people from the NBC News bureau set up there, so we kept walking.

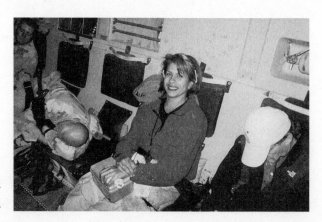

Aboard a C-17 en route to Baghdad

With producer Tim
Uehlinger in Baghdad

Shooting near the
downed statue of
Saddam Hussein

At last, a U.S. military vehicle stopped and gave us a ride into Baghdad. NBC had already outfitted a small building for crews and correspondents who were there before us. The space was geared for plugging in equipment and computers, and also for sleeping. On our first night, David Bloom's funeral was under way back in the states. NBC had rigged it so we could watch a satellite feed of the funeral inside our little compound. We sat in the dark to watch, because any extra light would draw attention to our building. Some of the correspondents worked by the light of headlamps strapped to their foreheads. There we were in the dark, watching the funeral. All of a sudden, "Pop-pop-pop-pop!"

Bullets.

Before we arrived, we were advised that whenever we heard gunfire we were to strap on the equipment we were provided. My gear was heaped in the corner—a helmet, a bulletproof vest, and a gas mask. My first instinct was to strap it all on—even the mask. But no one around me was moving. Not an inch. I looked around the room. *Really?* Everyone was just working on their stories and watching the funeral like nothing was wrong. Jim Maceda, a thirty-year news veteran who's covered stories in more than a hundred countries—many embroiled in conflict—looked toward the window where the gunfire was popping.

"Pop-pop-pop-pop!"

Completely annoyed, like he was hearing a swarm of gnats instead of a flurry of bullets, he said to the window, "Shut the *fuck* up!" He turned back to his computer and continued writing his story. I was amazed that the same sounds I found terrifying were simply an irritant to the wizened war veteran. I saw it again a few days later.

I was interviewing a woman who headed up the hospitals in Baghdad. She was understandably distraught over the bombing chaos. Medical records, blood-type information, birth certificates—all strewn about and many destroyed. We were outside in the hospital courtyard when the same "Pop-pop-pop-pop!" kicked in. She didn't flinch or even stop talking. I, on the other hand, was thinking about all my gear again. She reached down into the sea of white papers, telling me how "this is somebody's records and we will never get them organized in time—"

"Pop-pop-pop-pop!"

Never skipping a beat, she continued, "—and especially we must get everyone's birth certificates located and children need medicine—"

"Bang-bang-bang-bang!"

I could've used some medicine. My mind was scrambling. *Should I hit the ground? Shouldn't I have my helmet on?! Why is this sixty-five-year-old woman just standing here?!* My blatant cowering finally woke her up to the noise.

"Ohhhhhhh—shooting—okay. Come on." She took my hand and dragged me off like I was three, and I gladly followed.

The next day, I needed to shoot what's known in TV as a "stand-up" for a story. That's when you see a reporter standing somewhere, talking about something. I wanted the shot to be colorful and remembered a fruit stand we'd passed by earlier. I told the photographer I wanted to shoot my stand-up there, in the market. I had no idea what a geographical blunder I'd made. Not knowing the lay of the land nearly cost me and my crew *big*. I didn't fully understand that there are no clear lines that mark dangerous areas from safe areas. (I knew how to breathe through a sack, but darn it, this one I had to learn the hard way.) We pulled into the market, which was located in an area dominated by Shi'a Muslims—the more conservative members of the Islam faith. As it turns out, while we would've been safe just two blocks away, on this block, we were not.

My sleeves were the problem. They weren't short sleeves, but they were three-quarter-length. It was hot that day. We got out of the car to shoot the stand-up, and I instantly got a bad vibe. Something was not right. My colorful backdrop was about to turn into a very bad scene. Someone yelled something, then a group of people started chasing us. I've never moved so fast. I jumped in the car just as my crew was jamming it into reverse and peeling out of there. In the frantic leap, I lost a shoe. I lost a notebook. Who knows what else we came close to losing. It was hairy—and it was my fault. "Oh, where's that pretty fruit stand? We need some color." What an ass. An ass with the wrong sleeves in the wrong area. We got it good from the bureau chief when we got back.

"What were you thinking? Going in there wearing *that*?!" It was a dangerous lesson learned.

Burma

When *Dateline* asked me to fly to Burma in 2000, I thought, *Someone find me a damn globe.*

Just in case you're not sure where Burma is either, it's the country bordered by China, Laos, Thailand, Bangladesh, India—you get the region. They wanted me to bring back two stories: One was about an odd set of ten-year-old twins who'd appeared on the cover of the *New York Times,* smoking cigars. They were said to have magical powers. The second story involved interviewing a female Nobel laureate who was locked away under house arrest. I'll tell you right now, we never found those twins. The story we brought back was instead about our two-day search led by rebel soldiers through the dense jungle—a Burmese "Where's Waldoes" of sorts. The story that did pan out was that of the imprisoned woman.

Aung San Suu Kyi hadn't done an interview in eleven years. Plenty of people had tried. *Dateline* wanted me to try, too. We flew to Burma once, but failed to set up a meeting. Ten days later, we got the okay and returned for a very dangerous interview. The challenge was that Suu Kyi was under house arrest in Burma. The ruling military party had labeled her a threat to the country's peace and security. Her father was General Aung San, the founder of modern Burma.

His dream was for democracy, but when Suu Kyi was just two years old, he was assassinated. Although her mother, too, was a diplomat and a strong supporter of public service, Suu Kyi grew up to want a different life. She chose to become a wife and mother in England for sixteen years. But, in 1988, events on the other side of the world would turn Suu Kyi's personal world upside down.

Her mother suddenly had a stroke in Burma (renamed Myanmar by current military rulers). Suu Kyi traveled to be by her side and found the country in turmoil—millions demonstrating for democracy. The passion stirred her soul. She decided to stay and help launch an organized political rebellion. She chose her country over life with her beloved husband and two sons, just eleven and fifteen years old. Within a year, Suu Kyi's drive and millions of followers were seen by the military dictators as too dangerous, and they placed her under house arrest. Military Intelligence cut her phone lines, stopped her mail, and kept her under constant surveillance. If she left the house, two cars and two motorcycles would follow. No foreign journalists were allowed to interview her, and those who were caught trying were interrogated and imprisoned.

See our dilemma? We were warned up front that if we were revealed as U.S. journalists in Burma, we'd go to jail for seven years—a long, hard stay that would begin with a strip search. Gulp. So, the plan was for me and my producer, Maia Samuel, to have a convincing "cover." *Dateline* decided we should arrive as housewives on a silk-buying trip, armed with a touristy amateur video camera. The sneaky stuff was more complicated. Our clever folks devised a way for us to safely smuggle out (we hoped) the precious videotapes. In our shoes! They gave us each two James Bond-ified pairs. In one, they hollowed out the soles of the shoes. Just enough space for a mini DV cassette tape. The other pair was the type of Nike with the bubble in the heel.

They rigged that tiny cavity to conceal a tape as well. Now, we just hoped we'd have a reason to use all this stealthy gear.

Getting the interview with Suu Kyi was the biggest trick of all. She had no phone, no mail, no computer, and was watched 24/7. The only strategy was *not* a big confidence builder. We had to give a note to a guy on a horse, who took it to another guy, who was the uncle of someone who took notes to her once a week. Add to that, the United States has no presence in Burma, so if there was trouble, we were shit out of luck. Maia and I were to meet a cameraman there who was flying in from Australia. We arrived at a hotel bar, wearing our 007 shoes, and crammed a piece of paper into a pack of Marlboro Lights. We slid the smokes down the bar, the photog took them and read where to meet us—at the secret location.

(A lot of the "secret" has to remain just that. Because Suu Kyi's life is still at risk at the time of this publication, we have not and will not disclose details about our undercover journey to the interview location.)

Ironically, Suu Kyi chose Armed Forces Day in Burma for our meeting. Hardly familiar with the Burmese calendar, we froze at the shocking sight of military troops, tanks, and weaponry filling the streets. We thought we were done for! The roaming forces added a level of anxiety we didn't need. When we finally arrived at the secret spot, we were taken in through a back door. All the curtains in the room were closed, all the lights turned off. From the second we began the interview, I wanted it to be over. I hate to admit that, since we'd flown all the way over—twice—but the thought of *How are we going to get out of here alive?* was overwhelming.

We took precautions well before we arrived. Maia prepped me: "We *cannot* leave any pieces of paper behind to be found and traced back to us." We were constantly tearing up papers we didn't need. She also made sure all of our written questions were generic and could have been directed at anyone. If we ever got caught after the interview, we wanted the notes to say "husband" only, not "How did your husband handle the responsibility of raising your sons?" We were so very worried about the wording of the questions and our paper trail. We played the "What If" game a lot.

Suu Kyi was not nervous at all. She was completely centered, fully calm. And somehow, this petite woman exhibited tremendous power. She spoke to us for less than a half hour—passionate, unyielding, and astonishingly full of hope. I, on the other sweaty hand, was extremely jumpy as we were shuttled out the back door, not even able to feel excited that we'd snagged the story. Would we and these tapes make it out of the country safely?

The plan was to use decoy cars to safely exit our interview location. Because the military was buzzing around at all times, the strategy was to throw off troops by using multiple cars. Thank God we did. When our "plants" left the interview location and hopped into the first car, the military immediately trailed behind. The second decoy car took off next. Troops tailed that one, too. Third and fourth decoy cars—same response. We got into that fifth car, scared to death. Our *Housewives Go to Burma for Silk* video was cued up in the camera, ready to prove our harmlessness. The precious tapes hidden in our shoes, we hunched down as low as we could in the back of that speeding car, praying that our feet would save our ass.

Can you believe—no one followed us! Phew. One huge hurdle down, one monumental one to go: the airport metal detectors. The wild card was how touchy they were calibrated. Would our shoe cavities safely conceal our treasures? My mind was racing, imagining the metal detector not only sounding an alarm, but blaring *"Strip Search!"* too. I was terrified and so was my well-heeled producer.

I can't tell you how *huge* of a step I took through that metal detector. *Like I was crossing a burning moat.* It worked! I got through. I turned around to see Maia, holding our video camera and showing officials ridiculous shots of us waving and smiling and pointing out touristy areas of interest. Lunacy. I'll never forget the panic in her eyes as she mouthed to me, *Don't you leave me!* If only I could show her the burning moat move! Thank God, she made it through the detector as well. Two housewives, two tapes, too damn scary. We got completely blitzed on the plane ride home. Relief by the glass.

How lucky we were to be safe and free. Suu Kyi remained a political prisoner. She was the first person I'd ever met whose priorities were so strongly and deliberately stacked against family life—in the name of her country and democracy. Even when the government offered her freedom to go home to be with her dying husband in England, Suu Kyi refused, concerned she would be denied reentry. For her choices (she will not call them sacrifices), she won the Nobel Peace Prize in 1991. Her eighteen-year-old son accepted on her behalf.

Afghanistan

I grew up watching Tom Brokaw on television. I was nineteen years old when he first began anchoring the *NBC Nightly News.* So, it was excitingly weird when I was asked in 2002 to be one of the correspondents for Brokaw's special, "America Remembers." The program would air on the one-year anniversary of the September 11 terrorist attacks on the World Trade Center. My role was to fly to Afghanistan in August, just ten months after Operation Enduring Freedom. That was the operation that unfolded four weeks after the 9/11 attacks. My valiant producer from the Burma assignment, Maia Samuel, and I would fly into Kabul, the capital city, and begin shooting stand-ups at various locations in the region where bin Laden, leader of Al-Qaeda, once worked and roamed.

I was exhausted by the time we landed in Kabul. Looking over the city from our hotel balcony, all I could see were dusty tanks, ravaged buildings, and the remains of mud-brick homes. The photographer who met us there, Sebastian (who looked like a hotter Jack Nicholson), said the structures had been so badly shot up by small-arms fire that they simply collapsed onto themselves. Somehow, weary residents had managed to reopen small shops offering inner tubes and bicycles or fresh fruit for sale. Anything to start over again despite the wreckage. Some of the women were still draped in burkas, but we did see a few small signs of change—kites flying, the sounds of outdated American music, bustling streets.

In the heart of Afghanistan

We headed out to shoot several stand-ups along the road from Kabul to the ancient city of Bagram. The Kabul-to-Bagram Southern Half Road, as it's known, is one of the major roads in Afghanistan. It starts in the Kabul district and ends, after about 30 miles, at Bagram Air Field. Both shoulders of that long road had a nasty little secret. *If* you were lucky—each and every one of those secrets had been revealed and marked with a small red stone. Underneath the stone was a land mine. Demining crews had done their best to identify the hot spots and alert passersby with that very primitive but effective painted-stone system.

When you travel to a foreign country as a television crew, you always hire what's known as a "fixer." He or she is someone who knows the local area, knows how to talk to the military, translates the language, knows what areas are safe, knows where to get lunch, and all that invaluable stuff. Our fixer was named Hamid. He was a great guy and told us how one day he'd been arrested by the Taliban just for wearing a hat during prayer time. Hamid was with us as we prepared to shoot a stand-up near a tank off the Southern Half Road. We'd asked Hamid if that stretch was mined, and he told us no.

Honestly, I had my doubts. Just a few days earlier, we'd picked a shooting location where Hamid assured us there were no mines. However, we drove by the same location the *next day* and saw demining crews laying down red stones in the exact same place. "This is where we shot!" I gasped, looking wide-eyed out the car window. Hamid apologized. So, with that mess-up in mind, I was very nervous at this latest location, tiptoeing behind our body guard as he stomped on any and all lumps to see if they were mines. (Isn't there a better system?!) The region was infested with them. Looking back, that seems so stupid—too risky.

Tracking bin Laden

Our next shooting location was the desert. There were camels everywhere, wandering and watching us. I shot another stand-up, this time near a nomadic tribe. There were so many beautiful children! If you spilled a box of marbles, you still wouldn't see all the colors that we saw in their eyes—ice blue, sea-foam green, cat's-eye yellow, deep emerald. I got so filthy during our desert shoot. Dust, dirt, and sand were everywhere. The baby wipes I rubbed across my face turned completely black.

The next day, we went back to Kabul to shoot along Chicken Street, a busy area with shops and outdoor markets. What a huge pain. As it turns out, the urge to say "Hi, Mom!" in whatever language is a constant around the world. Wherever we set up our camera, out came the crowds and waving hands. It took us forever to get a clean take. Our hotel was getting old, too. The toilets—though we were glad to have them—were filthy. The water only trickled, and the rooms felt like saunas in the 100-plus-degree temperatures. The good news was that we were leaving. The bad news? Sudan.

What a hole. Government minders followed us everywhere. Add to that 115-degree heat *and* the rainy season. We shot all day in primitive villages. I was amazed that somehow the children who lived there were smiling. With no balls or toys to play with, they kicked around old cans and glass bottles. They lived in huts side by side with the family goats. No water, no electricity. Whenever we took a photo of the children, they always wanted to stand near their cow—a status symbol—just like posing near the shiny new car.

We shot a stand-up on the road that bin Laden's construction company built, another by his office in Khartoum. The women there were dressed in striking colors: bright oranges, vibrant greens and reds. They covered only their hair, not their faces or eyes—a refreshing change from Kabul. Our stand-ups completed, we headed for Islamabad. I was tired and had lost some weight on the Pepcid AC diet. Ugh. I would've loved to have flown home to the United States from Islamabad, but that would've been a mistake.

I was just 300 miles away from a story heard round the world.

Pakistan

It's nearly impossible to imagine how a woman could overcome such a cruel, treacherous, violent attack. But somehow, Mukhtaran Mai did. She was the reason I didn't fly home. *Dateline* was now sending me to Pakistan to find her—a needle in a haystack in a tiny village in a time warp.

The good news for me was that they paired me with producer Tim Uehlinger. The guy is amazing. It's like he has an internal metal detector just for finding needles. And this was a story where even the haystack was hidden. I had to have *him* for a chance at finding *her*.

Tim was waiting for me in the Islamabad International Airport at three-twenty in the morning, waving wildly from a sea of galabeas, long white housedresses worn by men in the region. He was carrying a treat—a box of LUNA bars. We took two flights to get to our final destination: Multan, a relatively modern city in east-central Pakistan. I have never felt more oppressive heat in all my life. We piled into a car for a three-hour drive to a small town whose courthouse had become a lightning rod. Inside, in the hours ahead, a historic verdict was to be handed down. Media was gathered from all over the world. Villagers angry for opposite reasons were jammed into the small, supercharged square. The area was in full turmoil when we arrived. I made it out of the car but had to wrestle my way through the masses to interview a defense attorney who claimed his clients were being railroaded because of international pressure. He insisted the filed police report in the case was a fake. "Yes, police are also an agency of the state," he contended, "and this is all because of the pressure of the state." So much emotion, so much anger, so much riding on the verdict. We had to get out of there. We had to leave the chaos and find the woman who was at the center of it all.

Dateline told us Mukhtaran Mai lived somewhere in the Punjab region, an area of the world where the roots of civilization run staggeringly deep—nearly 4,000 years deep. As we drove farther and farther outside town, we realized not much had changed over those millennia. Tim had found us a police escort for two reasons: one, to point us in the direction of Mukhtaran's village some 100 miles away; and two, to keep us safe from bandits who roamed the lawless and sparse route. I'd use the word "roads," but that would be generous. Rugged and treacherous might be generous, too. I'll never forget the sight of a wooden cart caught in a deep crater, the donkey suspended in air. He was calm, as if it happened often, and simply hung from his cart like Max from the sled in *The Grinch Who Stole Christmas*.

Why were we trying to find Mukhtaran? Because her story had made headlines around the world. And we wanted to beat *20/20*. We'd heard they were on the trail, so our goal was twofold: beat the competition and tell this woman's incredible tale of survival and strength.

Two months earlier, thirty-year-old Mukhtaran had been raped—sadly, not a rare crime anywhere in the world, let alone in her small village of Meerwala. The reason this crime made news around the globe was that the local tribal council members in her village *ordered* Mukhtaran raped—*by* the members—as punishment for an alleged act committed by her twelve-year-old brother. Astounding. Fiendishly, the tribal councilmen had lured Mukhtaran and her father to them, claiming they needed her to simply apologize to a wealthier clan. Instead, they grabbed her and held her father at gunpoint. Fellow villagers looked on as she was led into a shed where she was raped repeatedly. After an hour, when the councilmen were finished, they stripped Mukhtaran and forced her to walk naked with her father and uncle through the village, assaulted once more by the screams and taunts of onlookers.

The rapes and naked walk were designed to bring so much shame to Mukhtaran that she would consider suicide and her family members would become outcasts in the village. For thousands of years in this region, women have been punished for the crimes of men, in this case, Mukhtaran's brother. He was accused of sleeping with an older woman from a wealthier clan. Dishonor to one family demands dishonor to the other, and often a female member is the pawn. This ancient tradition of justice is simply a way of life in the rural land. *But* the incredibly brutal nature of the punishment doled out by the tribal council caught the attention of a local imam. A few days after the rape, the Islamic leader publicly denounced the council's decision as "evil." Mukhtaran's shattered family found strength in the imam's support and reported the crime to police.

That was the game changer. That's when the terrible tale got what it needed to bring justice: *ink*. When Mukhtaran's story appeared in Pakistani newspapers, word of her gang rape quickly spread around the world. The story ignited outrage and put pressure on the Pakistani government to do something. Within two weeks, the tiny village of Meerwala—with no water, no power, no electricity—was crawling with investigators. Fourteen men were arrested, death by hanging the potential punishment.

(I should note, investigators also determined that Mukhtaran's brother never did sleep with the older woman from the wealthier clan, but was instead sodomized by men in the clan. When he threatened to report it, he was set up with the phony story.)

The pressure on Mukhtaran to remain silent was tremendous. She and her family were the target of constant death threats. Still, determined to see justice served, Mukhtaran took the rare step of publicly testifying about the gang rape. You can see why we'd want to search a desolate 110-degree plain for this strong, brave woman.

The oppressive heat felt extra hot to me, as I'd developed a 103-degree temperature upon landing in Multan. Dr. Tim had tracked down some sort of exotic pill cocktail for me and urged me to down it. Red, blue, randomly shaped and sized—he plopped all the pills in my hand and I popped them into my mouth. I'm normally pill averse. But I'd flown all the way to Pakistan and did *not* want to miss the story. Tim, once again finding what we needed, saved the day.

With our police escort, we headed out in a Jeep—Tim and I, two photographers, and a sound guy. The drive would take hours and hours, with no guarantee of finding Mukhtaran. We made an arrangement with police officials that once we got close to her village, they would point us in the right direction, then leave. We did not want to scare off Mukhtaran. Once we arrived in Meerwala, someone pointed to a hut and told us she was there. Somehow, in the middle of nowhere, we were exactly where we needed to be.

The first thing we saw were goats wandering outside in the yard. Then Mukhtaran's father standing by the door. I spoke a bit of universal Arabic to him. Sort of a "Hi, how 'ya doin." He extended his hand and we shook hello. He led us inside, where we met the family, including Mukhtaran. She was covered from head to toe, just her eyes revealed. Flies buzzed throughout the hut. At this point, you may be wondering: Why did he let us in? Weren't they suspicious of the media? The only way I can explain it is that our world is so far removed from the world they live in, they're just not familiar enough to feel afraid. They had been through hell in their neck of the woods. Whatever threat we may have presented just did not compute.

We spent a bit of time getting comfortable, meeting each family member and looking around the hut. Finally, we sat down with Mukhtaran, who agreed to be interviewed. As is the case whenever a translator is involved, the pace and flow of the conversation was a bit bumpy. And I couldn't fully see her eyes. Even the small slit she looked through was covered by another thin veil. Still, I could feel her and I liked her. She was timid by nature, not because of our presence. Knowing what she'd been through, I was completely amazed by her composure and strength to pursue her attackers.

"If I had my way, I would have subjected them to the same treatment," she said. "If they were human, would they have done this? They are animals." She quietly described the horror mixed with confusion. "I begged them for mercy. I kept praying to God," she said, "and when they didn't listen to me, I just prayed to God. I said 'God, you know that I haven't done anything wrong, so why is this happening to me? And do save me!'"

Mukhtaran's father agreed to speak as well, telling us how council members held a gun to his head as he watched men walk in and out of the shed. "What could I have done?" he explained. "I just prayed to God. There's nothing I could have done."

Our interview lasted about thirty minutes. We headed back outside into the blazing sun. Tim was constantly ringing out sweat from a red bandana tied around his forehead. I had to shoot a stand-up before we hit the road, and I kept fumbling. I could not get a clean take and was sweating like an ox. Finally, we finished and began the long trip back to Multan, then home.

Back in the Punjab provincial town of Dera Ghazi Khan, it was time for the verdict in Mukhtaran's trial. Hundreds of relatives and villagers had traveled the many miles to protest and pray outside the courthouse. Journalists from across the world awaited the decision. Armed police units erected barricades to hold back the restless crowd. Nothing happened fast. The trial extended well into the night. Mukhtaran had been advised to stay in her village, surrounded by police, when the verdict came down. We'd heard that angry clansmen had threatened to pour acid in the face of the brave imam who'd spoken up for Mukhtaran. In a special midnight session, jurors made their decision: death by hanging for six men involved in the gang rape. *Dateline* crews that remained behind captured Mukhtaran's relief.

"I think justice has been done. I hope that much good will come out of this decision. I'm praying that this becomes an example, and nobody else would dare touch another in this country, ever."

So many legal twists and turns have unfolded over the last eight years. As of this printing, Mukhtaran's attackers remain in prison but the death penalty has been dropped. Her case is pending. With the money she was awarded by the Pakistani government, Mukhtaran built two schools in her village—one for girls and one for boys. The girls' school, never an option for her, is the first ever in Meerwala. Money donated by supporters from around the world allowed Mukhtaran to create a women's welfare organization to promote safety and opportunity for women. In 2006, her autobiography was released in English, titled *In the Name of Honor*.

I love this endearing evolution—Mukhtaran's last name is actually Bibi, but she has come to be known as I have referred to her throughout: Mukhtaran Mai, which means "respected big sister."

Tsunami

"Oh, good, you're here," I heard, sitting in my office.

"We need you to go to Southeast Asia right away." Details of a horrible story unfolding there were flooding the newswires. I was told: "Hurry up and pack. There's a night flight and we'll need you to feed back tape as soon as you land because we'll have a show coming up." Damn. My producer and I were already behind—and we hadn't even left.

On the day after Christmas of 2004, a magnitude 9.3 earthquake struck off the northwest coast of the Indonesian island of Sumatra. The massive earthquake cracked open the ocean floor, launching the overlying water into a monster tsunami wave. The highest crest of the wave may have been as tall as 80 feet. An estimated 200,000 people were killed, including tourists from around the world and residents of thirteen countries.

There was no way for us to get to the area fast. Our trip began with an eighteen-hour flight to Bangkok, Thailand. Airborne, with no access to the breaking and changing news of the tsunami's aftermath, we were once again behind. When we finally landed, our emails reminded us to "Feed tape right way!" For goodness' sake, we just hoped we could locate our London-based crew upon arrival so we *could* shoot something.

Our next flight was aboard a twenty-seater plane, south to Phuket, an island off the west coast of Thailand. That's where we had to find stories, *fast*. My producer, Justin Balding, and I decided to split up on the plane so we could sit next to passengers who might have interesting tales to tell. That would give us the head start we needed. I sat down next to an Australian surfer. I asked him why he was headed for Phuket. He told me his friend had been in the tsunami. "Oh, really," I probed. "Yes," he said. "He was in a boat, and the boat went *up*, and then went *down*." Thankfully, he said his friend rode the big wave and was fine. My hunt continued for a better story, somewhere on that plane.

The surfer continued to chat, showing me photos on his computer. I could barely focus, looking at pictures of his grandmother but worrying about my deadline. Then a photo popped up and the surfer said, "Oh, there's my friend." The photo showed a man in a wheelchair. Hold up—this was the man who rode the wave out on a boat? Our surfer had failed to share with me that his friend was disabled, had no use of his legs, and while tethered to the side of the boat, actually pulled another stranded person from the water. *Now* we had a story. The minute we landed, I asked him to call his friend. No answer. Panic. I asked him to try one more time. Success!

"Oh, hey, mate. I'm with someone from . . . Where are you from? American television and they want to interview you."

His friend said, "Sure, how about Wednesday?" I suggested in ten minutes.

"Okay."

We headed for the beach. A dinghy was popping across the water toward us. In the name of speed, I waded out into the water to meet our guy, the crew following, splish-splash. Bruno Hanson was a thirty-three-year-old yachtsman from South Africa. Tan, beach blond, and Matthew McConaughey–fit, he looked completely seaworthy. He told us how, on that sparkling morning of December 26, he was sitting aboard his 50-foot catamaran moored in the shallow waters off Phuket when all of a sudden the cat dropped 10 feet in the water and began spinning out of control. Confused, Bruno had no idea what was happening as he clung to his wheelchair.

"I was in the chair," he said, "and I jumped over to the seat where I sit to control everything."

That's when he saw it—the monster wave, barreling down on him.

"It was horrific. I just sat there. I didn't know what to do."

The water's impact knocked him to the floor and he began to crawl. What a helpless feeling for anyone, let alone a man paralyzed from the waist down. Six years earlier, a car accident took his legs and now a killer wave was threatening to take his life. That's why it's even more amazing that this man, who somehow tethered himself to the boat, was able to pluck another man from the water who was clinging to a jet ski. Bruno and his grateful passenger watched in awe as the wave swallowed up the shoreline, hungry for more.

"Cars were being flipped, people were screaming," he described. "Bodies were getting washed everywhere."

We raced back to dry land and began writing what would be the first story we fed back to our hungry *Dateline* producers. (By the way, we and other journalists on the scene were lined up on the side of a mountain, desperate to feed our videotapes. A Turkish guy was the only one in the area who had a working satellite dish. He did *not* know what hit him. Reporters from all over the world were begging him to feed faster in order to keep the line moving. Those pesky deadlines . . .)

Our hunt for more compelling stories took us to one of the island's hospitals. There we met a man missing one of the two most important things in his life: his youngest daughter. Steve Fitzgerald had two girls, and while one was safe, the other was nowhere to be found. Twenty-one-year-old Anna and twenty-three-year-old Kate had been vacationing in tropical Phuket when the tsunami hit. The two were hunkered down in a bathroom and were literally snatched up by the wave and tossed into the mayhem. Like so many others, the girls fell victim to the water's fast and ferocious attack. Once Steve flew in from South Africa, it took him eighteen agonizing hours to get any word on his daughters: Kate was in the hospital; but Anna, a business student in her final year of college, was missing.

Where to begin? As you can imagine, there were constant reports of survivors and bodies being found. Steve raced to every location that held promising news. He put up flyers. He even identified bodies at makeshift morgues around the island. An aid worker told Steve he thought he saw Anna's name on a hospital log. But each time, no Anna. "You can't have the luxury of thinking about your past with your daughter or contemplation of your life or your lack of life going forward," he reasoned. "You just deal with what you can do now to try to find your daughter."

Imagine the horror of having to peek inside body bags, not even sure what you're hoping to see. Which is worse? The agony of never knowing? Or the horror of reality staring you in the face? After too many days passed, Steve began to realize he'd lost Anna. "At her twenty-first birthday recently, I said that I didn't know of many parents who could say that after twenty-one years," he said softly, "their child hadn't given them one single moment of problems. That was my child." His head dropped into his hand like a lead weight and he began to sob. I asked Steve, in this unthinkable situation, what he said to God.

He just looked at me—for a long time. I thought maybe he didn't want to answer the question. Finally, he said, "What do I say to God? I say, 'Thank you.'"

"Thank you?" I asked.

"Yes. Thank you for not taking both of them," he said.

Boy. I was not expecting that. I remember thinking, *I can't believe what people can withstand.* How could this man retain the right perspective, the grace of gratitude? I was so blown away—and so *not* excited about what I knew I had to do next. I had to get the tape fed for *Dateline.* I had to get up immediately and walk out of that room. Every reporter faces these horribly awkward moments that deadlines create. There's just no easy or smooth way to say to someone whose heart is on the table, "I've got to go." The reality is this: You realize you've gotten what you need for the story, the damn clock is ticking, and leaving is the only way you're going to get this person's important words on the air. So you strip off your microphone and head for the door. That's how it was in Phuket with Steve Fitzgerald. I simply had to cut this poignant, painful moment short. I hugged him and hoped he understood. How could he understand anything that was happening? Nothing made sense in Phuket at the moment.

In the final segment of our tsunami series, we featured a married couple from Toms River, New Jersey. They were inseparable, married for thirty-three years. What brought Ed and Helen Muesch to Thailand was a round-the-world boat rally. Theirs was one of twelve boats gathered at Phi Phi Don, a small island fifteen miles off Phuket. The plan was for all the rally friends to celebrate Christmas Day together.

When I met Ed, he was walking with a cane. And he was rattled. He was still trying to process how the beautiful memories he and his wife had set out to create were literally washed away, and why he was forced to make a decision that would haunt him for the rest of his life. Visibly tired, Ed began to describe the wave's sneak attack.

Just before eleven o'clock in the morning, Ed and Helen returned from breakfast on Phi Phi Don. They were headed back to the beach to get their inflatable and board their boat. But strangely, when they arrived at the beach, there was barely any water left where the boats were anchored. How could it be? The boat was floating in 40 feet of water when they left. As they dragged their inflatable across the exposed sand to reach water, skippers in Thai canoes were waving them back and jumping from their vessels. In the distance, Ed said he made out what looked like a small foam line on the horizon. He and Helen decided to abandon the dinghy and head back to the beach.

"We held hands and we started running really fast," he recalled. "The wave wasn't that tall, but it was this white, foaming froth."

The boiling wave gained on them with tremendous speed. Ed and Helen were driven underwater by its pressure and brute force. Now submerged, he described the water above them as stewing with debris and bodies. Neither could get air. Twirled and tumbled by the angry froth, the couple ended up on the other side of the island. Ed realized, in terror, that they were getting pulled back out to sea. Helen was unconscious and just out of his reach.

"I tried to get up and she slipped away from me," he said. "My hand grabbed a piece of pipe and I was able to pull my head above water."

Sucking in a huge breath of air, Ed reached down for Helen and brought her up. Pure white. That's how he described his wife's face. She was barely breathing. Clawing about for safety, Ed somehow grasped the propeller shaft of a Thai canoe. A dazed man standing in the boat seemed oblivious to Ed's screams for help. He begged the man to help him get Helen aboard. Finally, the man came to life and helped yank Helen into the boat. Ed scrambled up and in next. Holding tightly to his wife, Ed was horrified by the view. Drowned people floated past, along with broken boats and random debris. Survivors were clinging to whatever they could with barely any strength left. In all the chaos, Ed was faced with a cruel choice in the form of a board. A simple, wooden board had presented him with the most complex and heart-wrenching decision of his life.

As Ed was screaming at Helen, trying to will her back to life, a desperate woman in the water reached out for him with a long, wet board. He was her only hope. Ed tried to grab the board, but it was too short. And he couldn't let go of Helen. He said he reasoned, "If I don't jump in, this woman will die. But I can't jump in because if I leave Helen, she'll die." Ed was crushed. "I made the choice *not* to go in the water."

With the help of a series of spared boats, Ed managed to get Helen to the hospital, where she barely survived. She spent two days in Intensive Care, developed pneumonia, and battled a heart infection. Still, she pulled through. Helen was weak but full of life when we interviewed her from her hospital bed.

"I would have drowned. I would be out at sea for sure. He has to take care of me for the rest of my life." She smiled. "That's the rule. If you save someone's life, you're responsible."

The lives he didn't save are what will always haunt Ed. I could read it on his face and in his answer when I asked, "What did you lose that day?" A long pause.

"I would say, self-respect." In his anguish, Ed said he sought out a crisis counselor on the island. "I just wanted one person to hear my story and really understand." He added sadly, "I didn't need anybody to forgive me, because the people who had to forgive me are gone."

Cruel. I looked down at Ed's cane. It clearly relieved only the smallest part of his pain.

As we left the island, it was amazing to see how soon after the tsunami people were again enjoying Phuket's beaches. Wasn't that disrespectful to all who'd so recently lost their lives? People I asked said no. They saw the flip side—the sunny side—the appreciation of being alive.

That's the lesson, I imagine. Like a huge wave that barrels across the ocean, or a gentle wave that laps the shore, there is an undeniable ebb and flow to life. I try to remember that. Move forward, move forward, move forward.

7

MS. GROVES

One of my dreams has always been to become a teacher. Because of *Dateline,* I got a rare ride on a neighboring cloud next to a woman who thought teaching would be heavenly, too.

I got the story assignment by default. *Dateline* correspondent Sara James had initially pitched the idea: follow someone in the Teach For America program during her first year instructing in a low-income community. The nonprofit organization was well established, created in 1990 to encourage people to teach in underserved areas. The idea required some cajoling of management because the financial commitment would be large. The budget would include daily camera work and frequent flights to the story site for producers and talent. Plus, what about the payoff? Would twelve months in school be interesting enough to watch? The bosses bit, but Sara's daughter became ill, so she could not take the story. *Dateline* passed it on to me.

The time frame would cover the school year August 2004 to May of

2005. The focus of our story was twenty-one-year-old Monica Groves, who agreed to begin her teaching career in Atlanta at Jean Childs Young Middle School. She had graduated from the University of Virginia, was accepted into the program, and was very excited to meet the children. I flew to Atlanta and met Monica in her new classroom. I liked her instantly. She was an optimist, a real glass-half-full girl.

"I'm so excited about meeting my students," she bubbled. "I haven't met them yet, but I already love them."

Our challenge was going to be our presence. Or our omnipresence, I should say. We would need to fill the classroom with cameras and microphones—all the things that make people nervous. Our hope was that after a while we'd become invisible. There were no guarantees on what we'd capture, but we were pretty sure any teacher's first year would involve some trials and tribulations. Monica would teach English to eighty-three sixth-graders. She and they were all African American, but beyond that, they didn't have much in common. She had grown up in a relatively privileged family; her students were not as fortunate. She was tiny at 5 feet 2, maybe 100 pounds; many of her kids were tall and big. Still, Monica believed love and enthusiasm would bridge all gaps.

Within a month, the water in her glass began to evaporate. The warm and fuzzy approach she'd taken was not working. Very few kids were listening to her or doing what she required. Homework was not getting done. Students were constantly showing up late. Kids were asleep at their desks. Monica kept working harder and harder but getting zero results. How could this be? In her mind, she was doing everything right, but everything in her classroom was going wrong. After two months, Ms. Groves decided to abandon Ms. Nice. Monica got angry. She yelled. And the more quiet she demanded from her students, the louder she got. This new stony approach to teaching came from a foreign and desperate place. And the worst part? It didn't work. Her students were *still* misbehaving and not learning. On her video diary one night in her bathrobe, she told the camera, "I am officially going through a tyrant stage. I spend more time yelling and correcting and discussing what we *can't* do than I do teaching."

Over the months, I would fly to Atlanta to interview Monica. I watched her agonize over all the things she was doing wrong. There was a time when she literally was beating her head up against a wall in frustration. Her dream of being the perfect teacher was as invisible as our cameras had become. And boy, were those cameras busy. Outside the classroom, we were taping an important aspect of Monica's kids—their troubled home lives. When an A student's grades began to plummet to D's and F's, we knew it was because her father had been sent to prison. When a boy whom Monica nominated for the gifted program didn't finish his final book report, we knew it was because his mom died, his dad was absent, and he was being raised by his elderly grandmother. When a B student with promise would not excel, we knew it was because his family was homeless and living in a hotel, five people to a tiny room. "Sometimes I do my homework in the car on the way to the hotel," the homeless student told our cameras. "Or sometimes I do it on the bed with my face turned to the wall so I don't get distracted." Monica was battling to overcome problems she knew nothing about. What she did know was that more than half her kids were being raised by single parents. Still, she had set a goal for her students that 80 percent would achieve a final grade of B or better. Four months into her teaching career, that goal was looking unattainable. "F, F, C, F, A, D, D, D, F, D . . ." she said, scanning grades from final exams for the semester. "This is just in one class. Not good."

In the middle: Ms. Groves

Monica's evolution as a teacher launched an internal revolution. Many times, she would cry during our interviews, exhausted from the Herculean effort with Pauper results. I asked her after semester finals how much gas was left in her tank. "I would say . . . about a quarter of a tank." She began to cry and choked out, "I love my kids and a lot of the stress I go through is me wanting to make sure I'm giving them everything they need . . . and me wanting to make sure I'm stepping up for them." Wiping away tears, she added, "It becomes a whole semester of 'not good enough, not good enough, you can do this better . . .' and it is emotionally draining." Monica was also struggling financially, making a very low wage. Socially, she was isolated. The classroom required all of Monica's energy. She also coached the cheerleading team and helped tutor kids after school. During one visit, we joined her for a typical night at home—eating ice cream and grading poorly done tests. "A 57. This is bad. This is really, really bad." More than half her kids scored a D or worse. "I keep asking myself, 'Did I set them up to fail? Did I not teach it well enough? Did I not give enough review?'"

Monica was overwhelmed and unimpressed by her own performance. She'd set a high bar for herself as a teacher. Over the months, I began to realize that the bar had a name. "I just want to be like Mrs. Kaminga," she'd lament. "I'm just not doing it like Mrs. Kaminga would want." Mrs. Kaminga was Monica's first-grade teacher. The kind of teacher she wanted to be. "Her demeanor was so supportive," she explained. "She just made you *want* to be better." The name would come up so frequently during our visits that I told my producer, Izhar Harpaz, we should begin looking for Mrs. Kaminga.

Toward the end of the year, there were still serious challenges. Monica found herself in the middle of a fist fight, Little Big Ms. Groves as they called her, trying to break it up. Thankfully, there were successes, too. The little girl's father was released from prison and he became involved in her education. The boy raised by his grandma made the honor roll and was accepted into the gifted program. There was a new home and a room of his own for the boy living in a hotel. He made the honor roll, too. After ten months of "baptism by fire," as Monica called it, she and her kids rose to the challenge. Eighty percent of her students achieved an overall grade of B or above. Monica found the "sweet spot" between a warm and a stern approach to teaching. She set up systems: "If you misbehave, I call your parents." And, "If you don't turn in assignments, your name and grades go up on a chart for all to see."

In May, on the last day of school, Monica was clearly exhausted from the long and winding road. We were together in her empty classroom as she packed up her things. And I had a secret. I knew that in a few minutes, the fabulous Mrs. Kaminga would walk through the door. Izhar found her, retired in Michigan.

I could hardly stand it. *What could be better than this right now? Nothing.*

Knock, knock, knock . . .

A woman walked a few steps into the room. She was white, which is a rare sight in this district. Monica looked up and said, "Hi."

"Hi, how are you?" answered the woman.

Again, Monica: "How are you doing?"

The woman said, "Well, do you know who I am?"

Still, *no* recognition. Monica hadn't seen her role-model teacher in sixteen years.

Then the teacher voice kicked in. And Mrs. Kaminga singsonged, "Can you thinnnnk baaaaack? Quite a fewwww years agoooooo . . ."

That's when Monica's eyes became the eyes of a child. Both hands flew up to her mouth. "Oh my gosh!" Then she burst into little-girl tears.

"Oh my God! Mrs. Kaminga! [sob, sob, sob] I remember what it was like to be in your classroom . . . if I could ever achieve that (tears) I would be so . . ."

Okay, look—very rarely do you ever get a *real* moment when you try to plan for it. Especially in television. Something inevitably goes wrong. Something unexpected interferes. But *this* was the real deal. *This* was one of those moments that actually worked. I can't believe I was lucky enough to watch it unfold. And I was bawling like a little girl, too.

Mrs. Kaminga threw her arms around Monica and rocked her back and forth, patting her on the back. "You willllllll," she said in that first-grade teacher voice. "I have noooooo doubt (pat-pat-pat)."

Rarely do any of us get the exact medicine we need at the exact moment we need it.

Monica Groves did.

We decided to call the series "The Education of Ms. Groves." It made perfect sense, since she was the one, in the end, who learned the most. The lesson was that you can work as hard as you possibly can and give your best and still not hit the mark. The story generated a flood of responses urging teacher appreciation and a lot of interest in Monica from talent agents. She chose instead to go back to graduate school for a master's degree and to return to Jean Childs Young Middle School to teach.

To our surprise, the raw, no-frills, not-sexy story of a year in the life of a public school teacher won *Dateline* two of the most sought-after awards in our business. "The Education of Ms. Groves" landed a 2006 Peabody Award and a 2008 Alfred I. duPont Award. It was a story that didn't originate on a battlefield or at a crime scene—the kind of compelling or dramatic roots you'd think would be required to garner an award. But it struck a nerve. It made people feel something. The education of Ms. Kotb was that even the ordinary can be extraordinary. You just have to look a little harder, lean in a little closer.

And I still want to be a teacher.

8

DATELINE

On the fourth floor of 30 Rock sit some of the best writers and producers in the business. Before I worked there, I was a viewer of *Dateline,* caught up in the whodunit stories packed with intriguing characters. But when I began work as a correspondent in April of 1998, I started actually reading the scripts written by my colleagues. The prose is genius. And humbling. Practically every time I write a script, I wonder why the hell I'm there. The biggest genius of all, phrase for phrase, is *Dateline* correspondent Dennis Murphy. You can pull up any Murphy script and want to steal everything in it. You can't believe what you're reading.

I remember what came forth from his fingers in April of 1999. Dennis wrote a script for a story on an outdoor memorial service for victims of the Columbine High School shooting rampage. The video began with a shot of a large, tolling bell. His line was, "If a breaking heart could make a sound, it would probably sound like this." Dennis delivers like that on every story he covers. In October of 2002, the so-called Beltway Snipers were arrested. John Allen Muhammad and his teenage accomplice, Lee Boyd Malvo, were caught sleeping in their blue 1990 Chevrolet Caprice at a rest stop off I-70 in Frederick County, Maryland (near the town of Myersville). In the course of twenty-three days, the snipers killed 10 and injured 13 people by firing shots from the trunk of their car through a small hole created for that purpose. *Dateline* had covered the story from the day the shootings began. Now, Dennis was covering the breaking follow-up arrests of the two snipers. The "perp walk" was featured off the top of the story, the middle recapped the three-week reign of terror, and the end showcased the "wrap-up." During the middle part, Dennis explained how the snipers left a sinister note at one of the shooting locations that read, "Your children aren't safe. Not anytime, not anywhere." Police collected it as evidence. With deadline pressure looming, Dennis had to wrap up the story. He probably yawned when he tapped out this about the day's arrests:

> MURPHY: Oh, and remember their note that read, "Your children aren't safe. Not anytime, not anywhere." (pause) Not anymore.

The guy is so good. I always ask how he does it, like I'm begging an Italian grandmother for her secret marinara recipe. He always says something like, "Ah. It's just drivel."

When I started as a *Dateline* correspondent, all the *firsts* were challenging. I'll never forget the day I shot my first stand-up for a story. Already nervous, I drove myself to the location, only to find that the street I needed to be on was blocked. I panicked. Turned out, the street was blocked off *for* my stand-up! When I finally got through, the street was filled with equipment that crews had spent hours setting up: a jib, a dolly, floodlights—an entire house was lit up. Coming from local TV, I was completely unfamiliar with this kind of *ta-da* just for a stand-up. All I could think was, "I better not screw this up."

During a *Dateline* shoot, the room can get pretty crowded—I didn't anticipate that. Often, the *Dateline* subject has his or her attorney sitting in the adjacent chair. That was the case when I went to Rikers Island to interview a schoolteacher who was accused of murdering her husband, a Staten Island firefighter. She had her attorney sitting next to her, and they constantly got up and conferred in private after I asked a question. When we interview a company or corporation, the room can get really tight. There's me, the interview subject, our two cameras, sound, lights, and then the subject's crew of photographers and audio folks. They will sometimes videotape us videotaping them for legal reasons. I'm always amazed in those instances by how "intimate" the interview actually appears on TV.

A lesson I learned early on was to simply check my ego at the door of the *Dateline* offices. Once you get a glimpse into the minds and methods there, you realize why the program wins so many awards and how its people put out such a great product. Simply getting a script on the air is an impressive process. Here's how it works: Once I finish covering a story, my producers and I get the first crack at writing a script. The next step is to head into a screening room with all the senior producers and the executive producer. We pop in the tape, everyone gets a copy of our script, and we screen the entire hour-long story. It can be agonizing to watch a room full of pens X-out sound bites and scratch through paragraphs. *Um . . . you know that paragraph right there that you scratched through? That took us five months.* More scratching, then the story comes to an end. The comments now begin from senior producers. "We're not in love with the main character," they'll say. Or, "I felt like that stuff in act one belongs in act two." Input comes in from around the room, tackling every line and every word. "I feel like we're missing the back story on that guy—I don't get him." And the dreaded "I just don't think we need that part." *You mean that part where we almost got shot?* We get a chance to defend our choices, and then the executive producer makes the final decision on revisions. We then get back to work, revamping the story based on the first screening. Next, it's time for the second screening. This one includes people from the Legal Department and the Standards and Practices Division. Gulp. These guys are like parents doing an inspection of their kid's bedroom—nothing gets by them. During this screening, Legal may say, "I don't think we should zoom in on that photo." Standards may offer input in the name of fairness. "You seemed to be more aggressive with him than you were with her." It's a great checks-and-balances system. And fresh, objective eyes always win. The process is long and arduous, but in the end, we're really proud of the story. Note that I didn't say *my* story. As you can see, it's in no way mine alone.

It's an honor to work at *Dateline*. I'm grateful. And one of these days, I'll get Dennis Murphy in the perfect head lock, and he'll cough up all his secret writing tricks.

Eyes in the back of your head, Murphy. I'm comin' for ya.

The Halls

Throughout the day, I see so many of my NBC colleagues in motion as we ride elevators and shuttle ourselves to various studios, offices, and conference rooms. One of my favorite people to pass in the halls of 30 Rock was always newsman Tim Russert.

Tim often came through New York from Washington, D.C., where he was the bureau chief and also the moderator of *Meet the Press*. Everyone loved Tim. He was incredibly smart and always made whomever he was talking to feel smarter. Humble and happy, Tim *loved* what he did. He would talk politics with anyone, anytime, anywhere—on and off the air. Professional but not polished, he'd run a comb through his hair and move on to the more important job of informing viewers. When he was in town and we had a live concert set up on the Plaza, Tim would come out and yell right along with everyone else, "Heeeeyyy, Bruuuuuuuce!" waving his arms at the stage where Springsteen was rocking.

Tim was Everyman, and you wished every man was more like him.

In June of 2008, I was spending time at my friend Bronwyn's house when a call came in from NBC. A news producer told me that Tim had died. I was utterly shocked. I thought, *But isn't he only in his fifties?* Tim was indeed only fifty-eight years old. He was at the D.C. bureau recording voiceovers for Sunday's *Meet the Press* broadcast when he collapsed, suffering a fatal heart attack. Five days later, his private funeral was held in Washington's Holy Trinity Catholic Church. I was flying out of LaGuardia on a one o'clock US Airways flight to attend the four o'clock private memorial service at the Kennedy Center. As I stood in line to check in, an airline staff member walked over to me and said he was in charge of the US Airways counter.

"Hi, I'm Mario," he said. "I'm so sorry about Tim. I loved him. When you travel to D.C. today, I want you to travel in Tim's seat."

I stood there as Mario took my hands in his. "Tim always sat in 1D," Mario said. "Today you fly like Tim."

I was so moved but not surprised that Tim had made an impression on Mario. He just had a way of letting everyone in—and everyone wanted to be there. When I landed, I was picked up by an NBC car service for the trip to the church. I got into the back seat and noticed the driver was crying. He said he'd occasionally driven Tim around D.C. for work and was saddened by his death.

I knew the church would be filled with dignitaries and people everyone would recognize. But how telling that before I even arrived, I met two regular guys who were just as affected by losing Tim. I feel fortunate to have crossed paths with him, even if it was most often in the hallways of 30 Rock.

9

NEW ORLEANS

The road to the network is paved with the call letters of local television stations. For me, they were WXVT-TV, WQAD-TV, and WINK-TV. WINK was located in Fort Myers, Florida, a lovely city along the state's southwest coast. In 1991, I was two-plus years into my work there, and it was time to move forward. I lined up two job interviews, one in Minneapolis and the other in New Orleans.

First was Minneapolis to KSTP-TV. I landed in the dead of winter—snow, ice, and freezing temperatures. The woman who picked me up at the airport assured me there were lots of underground tunnels that Minnesotans use to get around during the cold months. She was dressed in a blue business suit and was very efficient. She led me into the newsroom, which felt like a well-run bank—quiet, tidy, and safe. Hmm. I was certainly given a warm welcome, but any chemistry between me and the station was trapped in the deep freeze.

From there, I flew to New Orleans to WWL-TV. I'll tell you

The love affair begins

right now—the chemistry there was instant. That's the station where I fell in love. And like many love affairs, it began with a drink.

When I got off the plane, a jazz band was playing in the airport, each musician smiling and dressed in bright colors. A heavyset woman with long, Crystal Gayle hair came running up to me. "Hoda, is that yeee-eeewwwwwww? Ahm Gail Guidry and ahm here to greet ya!" (Insert big bear hug here.) Full of fun and chat, Gail took me to the station and into the WWL newsroom. There was lots of noise. People were high-fiving each other after beating the competition on a story, and desks were piled high with papers. Had I boarded the Mother Ship? This was my kind of chaos. That night my news-director-to-be, Joe Duke, drove me to an area just off the lively French Quarter. After a few blocks, he pulled into the drive-through lane of a Popeyes Chicken and Biscuits. I laughed uncomfortably, and he said, "You'll see. It's a *Super* Popeyes."

Joe into the speaker: "We'll have two chicken dinners . . . and two margaritas . . ."

Joe to me: "Do you want salt or no salt?"

My jaw dropped. *What? Drive-through margaritas? Wasn't this an interview?*

My new boss handed me a drink (in the car), without salt, and said, "Welcome to New Orleans."

I was in love.

Moss Man

Not long after I arrived at WWL, it was time for "the Big One." *The* story. Just one month into my job, Fat Tuesday graced the calendar in all its gaudy glory. Mardi Gras!

"You need to get an outfit," producers told me.

An outfit? Okay.

"Like a clown or something. Just pick something."

I picked a devil. The horns, the pitchfork, the red suit. I looked in the mirror, shrugged, and went to work as Beelzebub. That's where they started pouring screwdrivers. (You'd think the Popeyes episode would've helped buffer some of the shock here, but it didn't.) I was the devil, with a screwdriver in my hand. At work. About to go live on the air. As luck would have it, this is exactly how you cover Mardi Gras in New Orleans. My esteemed colleagues and I went live from the parade route in outrageous costumes, sipping drinks and letting the good times roll.

And then the wheels rolled right off.

During one of the morning live shots, I was chatting away when "something" came up behind me. It grabbed me and picked me up!

Then it started spinning me, twirling me around. *Live on the air!* Little did I know, Moss Man had engulfed me in his mossness. All I kept thinking was *I'm getting fired. One month in and I'm getting fired. We're live, I'm drinking, and I'm twirling in the air. I'm getting fired.*

When we finally got back to the station, I was ready to apologize immediately. But before I could, producers were yelling to me, "We ran that clip fifteen times! People can*not* get enough of that!" Once again, I thought, *Oh, Lord, I love this city!* To this day, especially when I'm in New Orleans, people still ask me, "What did you think about that Moss Man pickin' you up? Was it fun? Whad ya think?"

Another year, I was dressed up like a crawfish for a Mardi Gras parade. A photographer and I were headed to our location in a live truck when a call came over the two-way radio. "We've got a triple shooting," crackled the assignment desk. "Divert and go cover it." When we arrived at the murder scene, I took off as much of the

Moss Man

Craw-stume

Crawfish and WWL's Bill Capo

craw-stume as I could. The photographer and I got out of the truck and began to cover the horrible story. The coroner was inspecting the bodies and we started interviewing shocked bystanders. After several minutes, we heard again from the radio. "Okay, feed back that tape," the desk directed. "And go ahead to the parade." So, I put my head back on, and the claw. And I thought, *This is so weird.*

But that's the way it is in New Orleans—an absurd mix of crazy fun and tragic crime. Looking back, that mix is one of the strongest cords in my connection to the city. Laughter and tears, caring and corruption, black and white—they all blend and boil like a warm, spicy bowl of shrimp creole. Not surprisingly, "What is you?" was never an issue for me there. People are used to faces created by a colorful multicultural heritage: Creole, Cajun, Caribbean, African. The French Quarter is exotic as well, with its mixture of French, Spanish, and native architectural styles. And my name? Child's play. For God's sake, there is a street in New Orleans named Tchoupitoulas. They're gonna mess with "Hoda Kotb"? I don't tchink so.

Living there has helped me understand myself better. It's made me realize that imperfect is perfectly comfortable to me. Whether it's a city or my apartment, I feel most at home when things are somewhat flawed. Now please don't think I'm a slob—I'm not. I'm not dirty. Dirty is an old sandwich on your floor. I'm—messy. Messy is where you can't find your other shoe. Often. What's weird is that I don't really notice that I'm a disorganized mess until someone comes into my space.

"Hmm, what the hell time is it? All your clocks are wrong," a guest might point out.

And I think, *What time is it? If you'd noticed all my old calendars, you wouldn't even have bothered checking my clocks.*

What's the big deal? Life is an inexact science. I'll admit that sometimes messiness can be a time suck. I've spent a good chunk of my recent life asking cabbies to turn around and go back to my place, because, "Dammit! I left my BlackBerry again!" Followed a few minutes later by "Whoops! Found it." It was hiding in the Paleozoic layer of my cavernous bag, *not* to be confused with the Mesozoic where I *thought* it was buried. Someone actually thought they were doing me a favor a few years ago by giving me a purse with compartments. Thanks, but yuck.

Compartments, files, systems—not for me. Here's how I like my purse (and I swear I showed someone the contents the other day, and this is what came out): loose dollar bills, jam-packed wallet, a winter hat, a hardback novel, a thank-you card with a dog on it, Advil, one glove, a travel zip bag with 3-ounce bottles, mints, my checkbook, cough suppressant pills, a bottle of perfume, deodorant, contact lenses, a comb, an apple, and a Christmas ornament.

Yeah. That's my world.

When I take coats to the cleaners, I invariably score big. One coat I hadn't worn in two years had a $20 bill, a few singles, and a business card in the pocket. I *know* some of you are relating to this. I know my sister and mom are for sure. I will watch them tear apart a living room looking for something.

"*Where* is that cranberry lipstick?" Hala will demand—with that look.

Oh, Lord, I think to myself, *everybody buckle up.*

When I watch my mom work her kitchen, I see myself and Hala. Instead of shutting the upper or lower cabinet doors, she'll bob and weave around them. Hala and I duck and dodge, too. *You're just going to open them again—why close them?* But one woman's kitchen is another person's crime scene.

• • •

When I worked in New Orleans, I was sitting at a restaurant one morning eating breakfast with my dear friend Karen, when her phone rang.

"Hello?" Karen said. "Yeah, she's sitting right here with me." Karen handed me her cell and said that a colleague went to look for me at home because no one could reach me by phone.

"What's going on?" I asked. My coworker proceeded to tell me that my apartment had been ransacked! I was shocked—until they began listing their evidence.

"Your purse was on the ground with its contents strewn about."

Yeah . . .

"Your door was unlocked."

Yeah . . .

"Your keys were lying out."

Yeah . . .

"There was stuff everywhere." (The cabinets were probably open, too.)

Okay. And then what? You connected the dots to what? What *is* the problem?

They thought I was dead. But they were simply witnessing the art of imperfection.

I did have a bad habit in New Orleans of leaving my personal checkbooks around the WWL newsroom. My desk, the assignment desk, other people's desks. I can't explain or defend it—it just happened. So, as a little joke at my going-away party when I got my job in New York, my clever colleagues made a trip to Kinko's. They blew up one of my checks and had sandwich boards made for people to wear. News producer Tia Landry actually attached my real checks to her blow-up version and wrote "NSF" (nonsufficient funds). She wrote out others for $1,000,000. Priceless, right?

Check, please!

• • •

One might say that my current office at NBC is, well, flawed. I still feel sick to my stomach when I think about one particular incident that unfolded there. Remember the story I told you about earlier? When I was sent to Pakistan right after the September 11 terrorist attacks? Well, as you might imagine, I was rushing to get ready for my trip. So, naturally, I began jamming stuff under my desk. My theory was that if anyone walked by while I was overseas, my office would look decent. Keep in mind that I accumulate lots of papers, old scripts, old videotapes, work clothes, stuff that people send me, and other sundry items. Well, while I was gone, a horrible situation unfolded: A letter with anthrax in it was sent to the NBC offices. Many of the executives were told to clear out of their offices and relocate so an investigation and decontamination could begin. As fate would have it, one of the relocated staff members was then executive producer of *Dateline,* Neal Shapiro. He needed an office.

And guess whose office was available? Yep. The office of Miss Amiss. Imagine your boss being handed the master key to your Closet de Chaos. In Pakistan, when I received word of the "relocation," I began to calculate whether 7,000 miles was enough distance between me and New York City. All I could picture was Neal Shapiro attempting to maneuver around all of my shit. *How's he possibly going to carve out a place to use my mouse?!* I panicked.

I had flashbacks of a trick played on me at WINK-TV in Fort Myers. The five o'clock anchors secretly sent a photographer into my apartment for their weeklong "Disorganized!" series. They surprised me live on the air with the "home movie" of my domestic chaos. Are you sensing a theme here?

Anyway, poor Neal. During a very stressful time at NBC, he had to work in a landfill. I imagined him jiggling his knees around under my desk, trying to find a tiny piece of real estate, and then bending down—looking under there . . .

"What in the *hell*?" he'd blurt out.

Neal did manage to peck out an email to me (I'm sure from a contorted position) that read: "I'm sitting at your desk and can't seem to get tucked into it."

Something like that. I may have blocked out the exact words, but suffice it to say, just seeing his address pop up on my BlackBerry screen was horrifying. Neal is a genius at what he does and is also a little hard to read, so after I scanned the message, I felt a disturbing mix of humiliation and relief.

Neal, may I say again that I am *so* sorry. (And I think you may have left a Diet Coke can on my desk. C'mon. A little help?)

Suck the Head and Pinch the Tail

People who live in New Orleans like nothing better than to watch you get "deflowered" by a crawfish. They love the look on a newbie's face when all those legs and two black eyes approach the eater's mouth. "Suck the head and pinch the tail!" they yell, training and taunting at the same moment. I remember my first crawfish, and I've lost count of how many I've sucked and pinched or pinched and sucked over the years since then. At first, crawfish are intimidating—and then they're addicting. Sort of like the people of New Orleans. They'll throw you off a bit when you arrive. I was so confused when I moved to New Orleans and people would say, "Where you at?"

"Well, I'm *at* right here." (What?!) I would learn soon enough that "Where you at?" is simply "Hey, how you doin'?" I also learned that people in New Orleans desperately want you to love them and their city. "She *loved* that étouffée," they'd say, watching me scarf down a bowl. "She *loved* it!" It's almost like having an insecure friend who wants you to show her you love her again and again. And you're thinking, *This is the best city in the world. How could I not love it?*

Having felt the pulse of New Orleans with my own two fingers for years, I'm now very protective of the city. I cringe when I see a typical movie depiction of the Big Easy. *Oh, look—it's three dirty cops in a swamp.* Is there corruption? Is there crime? You bet. Just like in all large cities. New Orleans is just more transparent and open about it all. I've always preferred to focus on the city's strengths and the huge hearts of the people who live there. One Sunday while working at WWL, I was scheduled to give a speech about the news business. I was provided a street address but hadn't determined the exact location by the time I got into my car. Minutes later, I pulled up to a church. Oh—now I got it. I'd been asked to speak at a small, black church in a very rough part of town. We'd covered plenty of break-your-heart stories in the neighborhood. These congregants had been through a lot. As I walked up the steps, I began to feel overwhelmed. What could I possibly have to say to these resilient people, dressed in their lovely church clothes and fancy hats? I would normally talk about television and journalism, but somehow that seemed too shallow. When I walked up to the lectern, I looked out at the small crowd of about forty people and was speechless. I stood there in silence—and then I lost it. I stood up there and cried. That's clearly not what they signed up for; but I cried. I felt so ill prepared. Then, an old black woman sitting in the front pew began to clap slowly. In her stylish hat and with her delicate, aged hands, she sat there and clapped. Then she announced to me and the congregation, "It's okay, baby. You take all the time you need. We'll wait." That made me blubber even more.

The generous spirit of New Orleanians is admirable. I felt it from people who had everything and from those who had little. When I announced that I was leaving for the network in New York, people sent me the kindest gifts. One woman actually took the time to knit me a soft, warm blanket because she knew how cold it would get up north. I still get birthday cards from people there, more than a decade after I left. My connection with residents of that city is for life.

Karen

One of my favorite takeaways from New Orleans is a woman named Karen. (The same girl I was having breakfast with the morning people at work thought my apartment got rolled.) We met in 1993 at WWL when I was anchoring the ten o'clock news and Karen was anchoring overnight news updates. I loved her instantly. Karen Ronquillo is a drop-dead gorgeous, smart-as-a-whip, funny, caring woman who thinks she's a plain Jane. It makes zero sense, but it's an endearing quality because she has such a hilarious way of downplaying her extraordinary into ordinary.

"I feel fat. *Look* at these jeans. I ate a whole box of potato chips and I'm about to have another one . . . and I don't care . . . *and* I'm not working out."

But you still look like Miss America. What are you *possibly* talking about?!

Karen and I worked and lived in New Orleans at the same time for six years. We shared a love for the city and our jobs until, eventually, we both pursued new opportunities. I moved away first, to New York. Karen moved to Boston seven years later to coanchor a morning newscast. Miles don't matter. Barely a day goes by that we don't talk to each other. I hear from her almost every morning at 4 A.M. as she's

Karen and me, 2009

driving into work and I'm having my tea. This is a typical conversation: "*God!* A dead skunk should be pictured next to me on my driver's license!" Karen says, dodging early-morning critters. "*Dammit!*
I am driving through this hideous stink. What are all these skunks
doing out here?"

When you talk every day, that's the kind of ridiculous stuff you
discuss. Funny how the mundane is actually the glue that keeps
friendships alive. Time and distance have had no effect on the depth
of my friendship with Karen, because we've been caught up on each
other's daily life for nearly twenty years. Along with a simple shared
joy of knowing each other, one of the many reasons that Karen and I
are dear friends is that I've been lucky enough to be along for her ride,
checking off the milestones of her life. And she alongside me. I was
there when, as a WWL reporter, she spotted a handsome detective
working a crime scene.

"Hoda, he's sexy and looks like Hunter from the TV show!" she
told me excitedly when she got back to the station.

Hunter was actually John, now Karen's husband. I still remember
her running to show me the ring when John proposed. Later, I knew
of their struggle to conceive and then shared in their joy as they wel-
comed Catherine, their sweet daughter, into the world. Karen got to
know my boyfriend in New Orleans, watched me marry him, and was
there for me during my divorce. She's close with my mom, my sister,
my brother—the whole shebang of my world.

Karen is a big believer in living life with great depth. She loves
deeply, her faith is rock-solid, and her passion for joy is strong. That's
why she gives me so much grief when I seek out more angst than life
naturally serves up.

"Is that sad music? Turn it off," she'll demand over the phone.
"Are those damn journals open? Shut 'em." Karen prefers to listen to

her darling Bruce Springsteen or watch a movie like *Planes, Trains, and Automobiles* that makes her laugh. "Why are you going to that sad movie? Why don't you just go dive onto a hand grenade?"

This is the same girl, though, who I came across on her knees in my bedroom, praying to my dad and to Mother Teresa when I had a health scare. Karen is the whole ball of wax—someone you want in your life for the rest of your life. I think that's why we never have and never will exchange birthday or Christmas gifts. We know that our friendship *is* the gift. Or, maybe we're cheap asses. But I don't think so. I know she'll cringe when she reads this, but too bad. It's payback for how great she's been to me since Day One. Even now, with her busy life, she *always* makes time for me. If I'm having a lonely weekend, I'll call and say, "Hey, what are you guys doing this weekend?"

"Book it," she'll say. "Book it now." And then she'll call me the next day: "Did you book it?"

I know she has a lot going on—a daughter, a husband, a job—and there's probably a much better time for me to be dropping in on them. But she always says, "Book it." Every single time.

I can only hope I've been half the friend to Karen that she's been to me. When I make mistakes in my life, she stands by me. When I have a win, she celebrates it. And when I get on the bandwagon of something I *really* love, she rolls with it. For about a month, I talked ad nauseam about a book I'd read and fell in love with called *The Power of Now: A Guide to Spiritual Enlightenment*. I talked about the rewards of living *in the now* as if I'd found the Rosetta stone.

Karen's take on the concept, as we shared a public restroom in Boston, was "*In the now*, I'm pulling the toilet paper off the roll," I heard echoing from the next stall; "*In the now*, I'm flushing the toilet . . ."

That's exactly who I want in my life for the rest of my life.

I love you, Karen.

Big Easy, Big Personalities

Along with my best friend, in New Orleans I also met one of my favorite characters in the city. He was a Big Easy native named Harry Lee. Residents also called him Sheriff Lee. They elected him in 1979 and reelected him six more consecutive times. Lee, an outspoken Cajun-Chinese American who said it like he saw it, certainly had his share of controversy in office. That's one of the reasons why Harry got reelected so many times—New Orleanians like their politicians spicy.

Do you remember in 1991 when former governor Edwin Edwards was in a gubernatorial runoff debate with David Duke, the highly controversial neo-Nazi and former Ku Klux Klan leader also vying for the governorship? Local news anchor Norman Robinson was mediating the debate and said to the candidates, "We've heard you guys talk about how different you are, but what do you think you have in common?" Edwards, known as a lover of the ladies, answered, "The only thing we have in common is that we're both wizards beneath the sheets." The voters loved it and Edwards won reelection by a landslide.

Sheriff Harry Lee was *that* kind of voter's dream, and was as well-loved as his long-time city colleagues Harry Connick, Sr., the district attorney, and Frank Minyard, the city's coroner. The three men combined have served the citizens of New Orleans for more than ninety years. In every other city I've worked, the local politicians lived relatively low-key public lives. Not so in New Orleans. I remember the first time I walked into a nightclub and saw Frank Minyard on stage, blowing a trumpet. *My God, is that the coroner?* I thought. I would watch Harry Connick, Sr., prosecute one of the biggest cases in New Orleans, and then there he'd be, moonlighting as a crooner at a club in the French Quarter.

Harry Lee died in 2007 after a short battle with leukemia. To this day I'm reminded of him when I look at the several Harry Lee mag-

Wild about Harry (with his wife and son), Chinatown, New York City, 2004

nets on my refrigerator door. He had them made every year—the Fat
Harry one year, the Slimmed-Down Harry the next. He was such a
character, such an original. Several years ago, I had to fly back to New
Orleans to cover a murder mystery for *Dateline*. Part of our story
included an interview with Sheriff Harry Lee. When we wrapped up,
Harry said to me and my producer, Soraya Gage, "Hey, I wanna give
you two some Harry Lee dolls." Harry had look-alike dolls made that
year. He brought out a big box and gave it to us. We said our goodbyes
and threw the box into the trunk of our rental car. As usual, we raced
to the airport to make our flight back to New York. We dropped off
the car, boarded the flight, and watched as the mobile air bridge was
rolled away from the plane. All was going as planned, as we taxied
back from the gate. Then we felt a jolt. The pilots had put on the
brakes and the plane lurched forward. We began to feel the aircraft
changing directions—this time back toward the gate. We could see

that the ground crew was rerolling out the air bridge to the plane. *What is going on?* we wondered.

Imagine this sight: a Jefferson Parish sheriff's deputy came bounding up the steps of that air bridge and onto our plane. In his hands, the box of Harry Lee dolls! In our hurry, we had forgotten the dolls. Turns out, the rental car company had found them and called the sheriff. "Hoda left her dolls in the trunk, Sheriff. We got 'em." You have *got* to love that passion. Soraya still tells me how her sons used to fight over who got to be Superman and who got to be the beloved Harry Lee. Steven Seagal can relate. During an appearance on the *Today* show, Steven told me what it's like to live in the shadow of Harry Lee. He said that each year, Harry would ask him to ride aboard a Mardi Gras float with him. "I used to hate it," joked the action-movie superstar. He said that invariably people would yell from the crowd, "Who's the guy up there with Harry Lee?"

It's tough to top Harry. He was a big personality with an even bigger heart. Just ask my mom. Whenever he came across an article about me in a magazine or newspaper, Harry had a blown-up wall hanging made of the feature. He did it for my mom and sent her several over the years. Even after I left New Orleans. She still has two hanging in her apartment and one at our beach house. For me, he'd often send a beautiful framed poster celebrating that year's Mardi Gras. What a guy.

Right before I left New Orleans, Harry took me out to lunch at Commander's Palace in the Garden District. At the end of the meal, he stood up. The sheriff then proceeded to sing in front of everyone in the restaurant, a well-known tribute to his city.

"Do you know what it means, to miss New Orleans, and miss it each night and day . . . ?"

I had tears streaming down my face. Frankly, his version was not that great, but I was so overwhelmed by such a dear and genuine gesture. And yes, Harry, I *do* know what it means to miss New Orleans. After six years of waking up to the clip-clop of the buggy horses' hooves, walking to Croissant D'Or for incredible coffee, running along the banks of the Mississippi River, and watching men wear panty hose for Mardi Gras, my heart has given the city its key. Even now, when I fly in or out of New Orleans, the longing is palpable. My heart pounds.

That's why it broke so fully in 2005.

10

HURRICANE KATRINA

I have watched plenty of tragedy through a camera lens, but in 2005, for the first time, it was my job to tell horrible stories about the people I knew personally and loved dearly. That August, when Hurricane Katrina left her watermark on the Gulf Coast and all of history, I was working at the network in New York.

I was in California getting ready to interview Raquel Welch for *Dateline*. News of a building Hurricane Katrina was swirling about the airwaves and newswires. The monster storm's rage was directed right at New Orleans. I was calling my bosses at the same time they were calling me. I knew I had to immediately leave the West Coast and fly toward the storm. NBC knew New Orleans was my "backyard" and I could find my way around. If I needed, say, a boat in a pinch, I could get one. Nothing would keep me off that story, and only now can I say that I truly had no idea what a tale of terror it would become. (I never did interview Ms. Welch.)

The NBC News crew and I got to New Orleans by flying into nearby Baton Rouge and driving an hour and a half to the ravaged city. Our first stop was I-10 in Jefferson Parish, where rescue crews were dropping off people they'd plucked from rooftops and remote areas. It was simply a spot on the highway that became the epicenter of chaos for tens of thousands of people. Buses would stop by, load people up, and head off to somewhere—anyplace but there. The rain was pouring down, there were no bathrooms, there was no food, no water, no medical supplies. People had been stuck on that highway for days.

"Hoda?" A familiar face I couldn't place was suddenly standing next to me. "I'm the principal of Bonnabel High School. You spoke at our graduation." She gestured toward a woman slumped down on the ground. "My mom needs insulin." Then another man. "Hoda, I'm a cashier at Circle Food. My dad is over there . . ." There wasn't enough of anything and too much of everything awful. I knew these people— they were my neighbors, my friends.

Sitting on the road, hugging her knees, was a woman I didn't know but could tell was in very bad shape. Rocking back and forth, with each movement she repeated, "My baby . . . my baby . . . my baby . . ." I knelt down with her and after a while she told me what had happened. She said a bus had arrived on her patch of highway to carry away the young and the old. As the bus began loading in a panic, she handed her two-year-old boy to someone aboard so she could reach down and grab her other son's hand. She also grabbed a small plastic bag that held what Katrina hadn't swallowed. There was a crush of people. The bus doors closed, and no one heard her screams as she chased after the bus. It was gone.

I asked her where the bus was going, and she said the rule was that they were not telling. They couldn't have people asking to be on one bus or another. *I'm waiting for the bus to Baton Rouge because that's where my family went* was just not practical during all that chaos. They needed to get everyone off the highway and out of the area. I motioned for a police officer to come over. I knew crews couldn't help everyone, but I told him what the woman had told me. It hit home. He grabbed a Louisiana State Police sergeant and explained the situation. The sergeant sat down with the woman and reassured her he'd get her on the next bus. Then, instead, he took matters into his own hands. I guess he needed a win. (We all did.) He took the woman, her son, their dog, and the little bag of everything and sped off down the interstate. I just saw taillights and the cruiser, blue lights flashing, driving away past a sea of humanity. I thought, *What in the hell is happening?* I found out later that mom and baby were reunited in Houston.

Surviving Katrina

• • •

Tim Uehlinger and I were working together on the Katrina coverage. (Remember Tim? He was with me during the adventure in Pakistan to find Mukhtaran Mai.) We did most of our reporting out of our rental car. It soon became a cluttered, stinky home base. We stored all our wet gear in there, we ate in there, and we were not showering. The only reason we didn't sleep in the car was that I knew someone at East Jefferson General Hospital. Graciously, she told us we could crash on the floor of a file room. Tim and I, as well as our photographer and our sound guy, were thankful to have a safe, dry place to sleep. We used old medical curtains for blankets. NBC eventually sent trailers for all the correspondents and crews, where we could rest and work.

In the first few days of our coverage, people on I-10 were lined up thirty deep—waiting. No sleep, no food, no water, no hope. As I sat in our stinkmobile, I could see a man trying to get my attention. He was yelling my name and holding up numbers. I didn't know what he wanted, but I knew he was desperate. Pointing at the numbers again, he mouthed, "Call my wife . . . tell her I love her!" I started dialing like a crazy woman. Punching the numbers. The call would not go through. Redialing—dead end, over and over. *Redial, dammit!* Tim had approached the car and saw me dialing and crying. He started crying. The whole scene was bad. He just looked at pathetic me and said, "Change your shirt. You've got to do a stand-up." He added, "God, you're sweating." Thanks, Tim.

I found a shirt somewhere in the back seat and started to wonder where I could change. Well, you *know* where. Right there. As I took off my shirt, I heard what sounded like the rumble of an idling bus. I looked up and out of the car window to see a bus full of people looking into *my* car window! Passengers were banging on the windows of the bus and yelling, "Hodie Kodie . . . we see your *titties!*" I burst out laughing! That weird hysterical guffawing when you're out of your mind from the absurd mixing with the horrible, and all you can do is throw your head back and laugh. That was me—topless Hodie Kodie. Thank God my friends were still funny and still laughing!

These were the same strong, fun people who were my angels when I was so scared on my first day at *Dateline*. I remember walking into 30 Rock with my new badge and there was some sort of problem. I was supposed to get buzzed in, but the guard didn't have my name. There was confusion and I was shaking. All of a sudden, out of no-where, I heard "Hoda? Is that yeeeewwwwww?" A tour group from Metairie, Louisiana, was gathered in the lobby. My people! I turned to that group of women and said, "I am *so* scared." Those ladies sprung into action. "You listen to me. You hold your head up. *You* are from New Orleans. You go in there and knock 'em dead!" My heart was in

Navigating the streets of New Orleans

my chest and they were holding me up and calming me down. I am forever grateful to those beautiful ladies. Once you live in and love New Orleans, the city grabs you by the roots and claims you as its own—no matter where you roam thereafter.

Back on the interstate, so many people were roaming and wandering—and hurting. We began to shoot a story we called "The Nomads." Sitting under an overpass, we spotted a group of four people slowly walking our way. There was a man and three women, one a teenage girl. They were sobbing. When they got close to us, we could see that their feet were making bloody footprints. "We haven't slept since Sunday," a worn-down woman cried, her daughter trying to console her. "We've been taking care of patients."

The nurses had been tending to hundreds of storm victims. When rescue crews arrived at their flooded hospital, they took the sick, but no one ever came back for the medical personnel. "It's just very disheartening," she explained, her big toe bloody and swollen, "that no one would come to help us." The four had stayed, waiting, until they realized that no one was coming. They set out on foot, and had walked for so long that their feet were raw and bloody. One of the nurses had a gash in his leg. He'd lost his home, was exhausted from caring for patients, and decided to simply start walking toward a relative's house 50 miles away in Tickfaw. "I'll get there sooner or later," he said with tears streaming down his face. "Can't take more than five or six days. I'll get my feet on some dry ground and see my family."

When an ambulance appeared in the distance, Tim ran out into the street to stop it. The sign on the side of the vehicle said it was from a particular parish. I gestured toward the nomads and said, "Hey, you need to take these people with you." The driver said, "We can't. It's against our policy right now." That's when I went nuts. Lost it. I yelled, "*Show* me the book. Show me the book you're using *today*—

for this!" They asked us where the nurses were going. "They're *going*," I insisted crazily, "wherever *you're* going. *That's* where they're going. Look at their feet!"

The ambulance workers finally let them in. Those four finally stopped walking. What didn't stop was the insanity. Or the rain. (To this day, my reporter notebooks from that trip are warped, pages curled from the stubborn, depressing rain.) A stone's throw from the French Quarter was my personal epicenter of insanity. Lying in the road, facedown, was a woman. She was dead. We must have driven by the body three or four times during our search for stories to tell. I kept thinking, *I can't believe someone is lying here, dead on the street, in the United States of America.* I knew crews couldn't get to everyone and they were triaging to get to the ones they could help, but . . . God. That image is seared into my brain. Did the people who loved her eventually find her? I barely slept. The struggle to maintain my journalistic "steel" was a challenge. Covering the destruction and sadness in the city I loved and watching my former neighbors' pain was draining, to say the least. At the end of one of my live shots for *Dateline*, the wheels began to come off. A talented editor had put together a gut-wrenching video montage of the devastation, set to Bruce Springsteen's "My City of Ruins." I watched it, my heart said "uncle," and the camera came back out to me live on the air. I begged my brain, *Please hold it together! You have got to hold it together.* The Human was sneak-attacking the Journalist. I was defenseless. I tried hard to focus on what I was doing, not what I was feeling. *You can feel later,* I repeated to my weak self. In my earpiece I heard, "Are you okay?" Kiss of death. Someone asks you if you're okay and the dam breaks. It was Steve Capus, president of NBC News. He was worried about me and all of his crews there. Was I okay? Yes, I was okay. I just desperately needed to see a tiny glimmer of something good.

That's when we met Sister Desiree Watson Jones. Sister? Was she a nun? I have no idea, but she was a godsend to me. "You need ice, baby?" she called out. "You need water?"

Desiree was trolling the streets of Jefferson Parish in a battered white Cadillac. It was jammed with emergency supplies that she'd talked a Federal Emergency Management Agency crew into letting her have. Her fiancé had loaned her the car for deliveries of ice, food, or clothes. The storm had blown out the back side window, now covered with a plastic bag and duct tape. "I could be in their shoes right now . . . exactly where they are," she told us. "Or even worse." This forty-six-year-old woman—an army of one—lifted my weary spirits. She simply went about the business of helping anyone and everyone she could find. If she couldn't provide material goods, she offered a kind word or prayer. Desiree took one look at me and Tim and homed right in on him, assuming he was homeless. (We were both *so* dirty and tired.) She handed him a piece of paper with her phone number. "I know you need some food, baby—you call me." He and I laugh about it now.

Desiree willingly popped on a halo and became an angel of mercy, even when she could've used some mercy herself. She'd lost her house in Jefferson Parish and all she owned in the storm. Earlier in the year, her son was killed in a drive-by shooting. Just three months ago, she'd had a heart attack. So much loss. What remained was her business, a tiny thrift shop in Jefferson Parish. Desiree was now living and sleeping in the Blessed Dressed Thrift Store. "If it wasn't for the thrift store, I'd have nowhere to sleep myself." Needy people crowded her storefront as she handed out all she could, no charge. Somehow, power had been restored to her little shop. She was a tiny bright spot in a very dark and dreary bayou.

• • •

Even the roaming Sister Desiree would have never found Gene Lala. He was out of sight, scared, and holed up in the attic of his house. And that's the last place you would normally find Gene, a New Orleans staple. Born and raised in the city, he's the guy who is first on the scene of every Mardi Gras and bellied up to the local bar telling stories. He is friends with everyone.

But there he was. Alone in his attic but for his beloved dog, Humbug. His house was located in the Lakeview area, hardest hit by flooding from the broken levees. As the water rose, the two kept moving up a floor. They were ultimately driven to the attic. Seventy-six years old, Gene salvaged two bottles of water and two bottles of Ensure. After three days and three nights, Gene heard a boat motoring around outside his house. His only option was not pleasant: take the dog and a deep breath, and swim under and out of a window, then up again to the boat. "Back in 1940," Gene said, "I was a brilliant swimmer. I used to swim in mile races. I never won any, but I swam in 'em and that was an accomplishment." And now, more than sixty years later, Gene swam again—this time for his life. Sheriff's deputies pulled him and Humbug into the rescue boat and asked Gene who they could call. Days earlier, Gene had dropped his wallet (where his phone numbers were) into the water. Lost. He had no children to call, no phone numbers for friends. He had only a credit card. Deputies had no choice but to take him to a nursing home in Baton Rouge. Humbug went with him.

Concerned friends eventually found Gene by tracking his credit card, charged to the nursing home. Humbug was so loved by the old folks, he stayed for a while at the home. Gene made it back to New Orleans, where he lived for months in a relative's gutted house with no walls. Humbug later rejoined him there. "Doesn't bother me," explained Gene. "I'd rather have no walls than a house full of water."

With his dog and a gun for protection, Gene lived in the ramshackle house for nine months, waiting for a government-issue trailer that eventually arrived. Gene now lives in a new, modular home also in the Lakeview area. His house of thirty-six years was destroyed forever, but Gene has what matters most—his life and little Humbug.

I've talked a lot about my love for the city of New Orleans, but after Katrina, I now redefine that sentiment as my love for the city's people. Thank God they are so resilient. New Orleans would simply be a dot on the map without them. They are the square peg that fits only in the square hole that is their fine city. No surprise, then, that just two months after the hurricane devastated the region, the food section of the *Times-Picayune* reached out to the heart—or rather the stomach—of beleaguered residents. The paper began a project to "rebuild, recipe by recipe." Because so many people had lost their cherished recipes to Katrina's appetite for destruction, the paper put out an APB for any and all recipes people could remember. With sweet irony, they came flooding in: red beans and rice, bananas foster pie, crawfish, and corn chowder. Eventually, a cookbook was created—what you could call the most delicious Lost & Found of all time.

I can't help myself—I just have to include Maria Vicknair's recipe from *Cooking Up a Storm* for one of my favorite New Orleans dishes:

BARBECUED SHRIMP

(Makes 8 to 10 servings)

1 to 1 ½ pounds butter

1 cup olive oil

¾ cup Worcestershire sauce

3 tablespoons cayenne pepper

½ teaspoon hot sauce

6 cloves garlic, coarsely chopped

¼ cup Italian seasoning

4 teaspoons paprika

¼ cup seasoned salt

6 bay leaves

4 lemons, cut in half

6 to 8 pounds medium or large shrimp with shells and heads on

French bread for serving

1. Preheat the broiler.

2. Put all the ingredients except the lemons and shrimp in a large saucepan. Squeeze the lemons, then add the rinds, too. Heat and stir the sauce ingredients together over medium heat until the butter is melted and everything is well blended.

3. Place the shrimp in a single layer on one or two large shallow baking or broiling pans, and pour the sauce mixture over them. Discard the lemon halves and bay leaves. Broil for 4 to 5 minutes on each side. When done, the shells should pull away from the shrimp.

4. Serve with warm French bread to soak up the sauce.

I go back to New Orleans several times a year for work, play, and barbecued shrimp. I do see improvement there, but I have revised my inner timetable to feel better about the rebuild. My friend Angela Hill, beloved news anchor at WWL, helped put it in perspective for me, helped reset my clock. "Yesterday, my mailman came back," she told me. "And it was a great day." A sign. A small sign of progress. The lesson is, don't look for a rebuilt highway, look for the mailman. Find strength and hope in the little victories.

I try to remember that when I go back to New Orleans. I try to remember how long it took for the Big Easy to ease its way into the unique spot that it is. I will wait. And it will marinate back into a rich stew of people and places, seasoned by time.

11

SUPER BOWL XLIV

On Monday, February 8, 2010, the front page of the *Times-Picayune* used just one word to speak for millions of people: "AMEN!"

Amen indeed. A prayer was answered and 106.5 million people watched it happen. I was lucky enough to be one of the thousands who got to see it unfold in person—to watch those New Orleans Saints go marching in to Miami's Sun Life Stadium and battle the Indianapolis Colts in Super Bowl XLIV. You've read enough now to know who I was rooting for, right?

The final stretch of the road to the Super Bowl was the night the Saints won the NFC Championship title against the Minnesota Vikings in the Superdome. I was in Florida watching the game (Did you hear me screaming from where you were watching?), and the moment the Saints won, our fourth-hour producer, Tammy Filler, emailed me to ask if I wanted to go to the Super Bowl. I warned her and everyone else from the get-go that I could *not* be objective. The ultimate decision-maker was my boss, Jim Bell, and (*Thank you, Jim!*) he agreed to send me. Hooray and Who dat! Over the next week, my phone exploded with emails, voicemails, and text messages from friends all over the country, and of course, from New Orleans.

I can't believe we're going to the biiiigggg daaaaance!!!!!!

It's oooooour time!!!!!!!!!! (Every message had repeating letters and exclamation points.)

My friend Matt, who was born and raised in New Orleans, held up his phone inside the Superdome the night of the victory. All I could hear was wild screaming. Other friends described how men and women on Canal Street were jumping out of their cars and doing "the Bus Stop" in the road. Strangers were hugging strangers. Music was blaring as car radios and boom boxes blasted the newly penned Saints anthems. Once again, the streets of New Orleans were flooded, but this time with elated, hopeful people. I could only imagine how nuts the scene would be in Miami. I packed up my black and gold, and left all my objectivity at home.

My dear friend Karen, whom I told you about, got her Boston news station to send her to our former home of New Orleans to cover the Super Bowl story, too. She was in heaven and sent me a fantastic photo of a priest wearing a Saints jersey, welcoming his flock into church. Most of the congregation was sporting black and gold gear, including "Breesus Christ" T-shirts. Can you imagine the prayers offered in churches throughout the city all week?

When I got to Miami on Friday night, I actually felt like I was in New Orleans. South Beach was Bourbon Street, and a sea of fleurs-de-lis greeted my eager eyes. Many people came up to say hello and share their joy with me. (And there were, as always, comments about that darn Mardi Gras Moss Man incident!) It was so much fun to mix it up with my old friends and neighbors, and to tap into an emotion we hadn't felt for so long: hope.

On the night of the game, we had access to the football field before the Super Bowl started. What an opportunity! My crew and I walked out onto that grass and just looked around at the crowd packing the stadium. The view was overwhelming—standing where the players would stand, seeing what they'd see during battle. For security reasons, I had to wear a bright yellow vest over my outfit while we were shooting on the field. But underneath, I was draped in Mardi Gras beads and black and gold, head to toe. I had to shoot a stand-up on the field, so I positioned myself with a sea of Saints fans behind me. At the very end of the stand-up, I ripped off that yellow security vest to reveal my true colors underneath. The crowd went nuts! "Hoda, we *know* you're for us! You don't have to hide it!" they screamed. It was hysterical.

Next, the game.

Covering a sporting event is never as much fun as watching it as a fan, because you're working and moving and missing a lot. So, I decided to plop down in a Saints section for a while and just shoot all that was going on around me before moving to the next location. There was so much energy to capture, so many highs and lows. I knew that sitting next to every Saints fan was a ghost—the ghost of the Ain'ts and of the four-decade-old cellar dweller. A lengthy past of loss creates a huge presence of anxiety. Every scream of "Who dat!" had a silent echo of, "Oh, no—here we go again."

I moved locations a few times and was also tracking down celebrities to sign a football I'd brought along from work. The idea was to get the ball signed by as many VIPs as possible, then auction it off to benefit the New Orleans Habitat for Humanity. (My thanks to Emmitt Smith, Archie Manning, Ashton Kutcher, Demi Moore,

At Super Bowl XLIV with hopeful fans

Chris Rock, Kim Kardashian, Kris Jenner, Bob Schieffer, and Atlanta housewife NeNe.) By the time the fourth quarter hit, I was again in the stands, elbow-to-elbow with worry-weary Saints fans. After a series of nail-biting convulsions and conversions, the Saints secured a 24-to-17 advantage. With less than four minutes left in the game, no one around me was willing to believe the Saints would maintain their lead to the end. Confidence would require every last tick of the clock. Then, in a remarkable split second, all the butterflies turned into sky-rockets. Saints cornerback Tracy Porter intercepted a pass by Colts quarterback Peyton Manning at the Saints 26-yard line! The elation was deafening as Porter returned the ball 74 yards for a touchdown!

All around me, people were crying. I hadn't seen men openly bawl like that over football since *Rudy* came out. It was a raw, unabashed tear fest and every Saints fan was in. If I had to put a word on the collective emotion, it was *relief*. So much doubt had been pent up inside, and now, all things repressed were being expressed in an explosion of joy. Wow! What an experience. After a successful extra point, with just 3 minutes and 12 seconds remaining, the Saints lead grew to 31 to 17.

My crew and I made our way out of the stands and scrambled down to the field with 25 seconds left in the game. Boy, New Orleanians are skeptical to the end. I couldn't believe how quiet the crowd was! Fans were not willing to fully celebrate until they saw double zeros on the clock. Only when Coach Sean Payton got his Gatorade shower did fans start to truly celebrate.

Because the Super Bowl was not an NBC-sponsored event, our access immediately following the game was limited. We'd been told that if we didn't race out to the center of the field, we would end up *outside* of a rope perimeter Security would create instantly around the players. Well, my crew and I strapped on our track shoes. The minute those seconds ticked down to zero, we sprinted. I may have posted a 4.3-second 40-yard dash. We made it inside the ropes, and then I just lost my mind. I stared up into the confetti blizzard and started screaming and waving my arms in the air. The photographer yelled to me, "What am I supposed to be shooting?" I shouted back, "I don't care! Anything you want! Point it everywhere!"

As luck would have it, I ended up crammed in next to the podium where the game's MVP, Saints quarterback Drew Brees, was hoisted and now waving to the cheering crowd. I was trying to get his attention, like everyone else, to ask him a question, but was having no luck. We were squeezed in together on the ground, surrounded by massive football players, the media and random people jammed into a very small area. Behind me, I heard a voice with a southern accent yell, "Hoda, git Drew! Git Drew!"

When I turned around, I recognized the face behind the voice—

Brittany Brees, Drew's beautiful wife. We'd never met, but I was delighted to see her. She was holding their adorable baby, Baylen, who had on a set of black head phones to protect his little eardrums.

"Just git'im, Hoda! Git Drew's attention!" she yelled, smiling at me.

My God. Here was the MVP to the MVP asking me for help. I started yelling my head off, cupping my hands to my mouth and screaming, *"Dreeeeeeewwwww! Dreeeeeeewwwww!"*

Nothing. My voice could not carry above the delicious din. Not even from the three feet I was standing from him. Then, an unbelievable call was made by my QB, Brittany, as she clutched the butterball.

"Hoda, peench his *butt*! Peench Drew's *butt*!" she demanded.

I stood there, frozen. "Um, what?"

She came back hard. "*Peench it!* I can't do it holding *him*," she said, nodding her head toward baby Baylen.

I must have been standing there in shock, because, again came the call. "*Goooooose* heem!"

Okay, I thought. *I guess I'm gonna have to take one for the team. I'm just gonna have to pinch Drew Brees's ass.* (Angels sing here.) And so, I reached up to the podium, grabbed ass, and twisted.

The play was complete.

Drew turned around to find out what the hell was going on and, thankfully, saw Brittany standing there with his son. She handed him that baby, he kissed her, and then he held Baylen in his arms. When tears started welling up in Drew's eyes, I realized I'd better start pinching myself, too. It was one of those moments when you just have to keep reminding yourself that you're watching history unfold before your very eyes. That you're right there—live. That it's happening. Don't miss a second. Watching Drew whisper into his son's ear, at one of the greatest moments of his life, was awesome. It was a moment for him, inside a moment for me, inside a moment for the entire country. The layers of emotion were as complex as the last five years of recovery for the weakened city of New Orleans.

The postgame party continued in the stadium for at least an hour. Saints fans did not want to leave. Everyone felt it. This was a public turning point. New Orleans got the right medicine for the right ailment. Right in front of millions of people. Somehow, the problem kid that they'd watched and supported for years and hoped would turn around finally did something brilliant. And everyone was there to bear witness.

"Who dat?!"

As long as I live, I will never forget the experience. Rarely in life do you get a front-row seat to the Full Circle Miracle. To have stood at the deep, dark, zero-degree mark of Katrina, then to share in the pure, sweet relief of victory 360 degrees later was an extraordinary gift. Whatever that night means or doesn't mean for you, for New Orleans, the Super Bowl victory is a building block—in the shape of the Lombardi Trophy. It's a solid foundation for optimism and confidence and strength. The city's years ahead will reveal the power that a fresh start can unleash.

P.S.

At a breakfast conference I went to in New Orleans fourteen years ago, well before Hurricane Katrina and Super Bowl XLIV, a dynamic speaker named Patricia Russell-McCloud stepped up to the podium. She shared a series of words that mean even more to me now than they did that morning.

She said, "If you fall—and trust me, you will—make sure you fall on your back. Because if you fall on your back, you can see *up*. And if you can *see* up, you can *get* up. And you can keep going and going and going."

Mrs. Russell-McCloud is right. Every now and then, when my life heads for horizontal, I pull out those four little words: *fall on your back*. And I try my hardest to land where I can see *up*.

Fall on your back. That advice sure helped me when 2007 rolled around.

PART THREE

Shit Storms and Silver Linings

12

THE BAD YEAR

Some kind of magic
Happens late at night
When the moon smiles down on me
And bathes me in its light
I fell asleep beneath you
In the tall blades of grass
When I woke the world was new
I never had to ask
It's a brand new day
The sun is shining
It's a brand new day
For the first time
In such a long, long time
I know
I'll be ok.

—*Joshua Radin*

I love music. For me, music is morning coffee. It's mood medicine. It's pure magic. A good song is like a good meal—I just want to inhale it and then share a bite with someone else. "Taste this!" I'm forever saying. "You've *got* to hear this. Listen to this line—can you believe it?" My friend Melissa Lonner faux complains, "You're always force-feeding me lyrics!"

I wake up at 4:00 in the morning for work and the music starts at 4:05. I go right for the *play* button on my countertop iHome. Sometimes I like mellow, sometimes I like Li'l Wayne. I pack up for work and head to the gym, where I crank forty-five minutes of high-energy music on my iPod. I could not work out without my tunes. If music didn't exist, I'd weigh 500 pounds.

At work, I have one of those portable iPod speaker things in my dressing room, which makes it easy for me to regale my NBC colleagues with good music. I like to bop into the makeup room with my music "purse" and watch the city gals with all their Versace and Gucci panic when they hear what's playing. "Oh, God, what is it?" they whine. And then I'll school them. "It's country. Put on your cowboy hat and shit-kickers." Then I'll crank "Hillbilly Bone" and hope they find *that hillbilly bone down deep inside.*

I love country and pop and R & B and some rap. I wish jazz had lyrics because I'm a words girl. Now, I do admit—I'm a song killer. I'll play a song over and over and over until it dies for me. I will *wear out* the *repeat* button on my iPod when I fall hard for a song. Then, by Wednesday I'm shocked: *How did I ever like that stupid song?* When I travel, I call ahead to make sure the hotel has an iPod docking station. I used to pack my *own* speakers to set up on the dresser, but since most hotels now accommodate iPods, I have room for an extra pair of shoes. I just feel naked without music. In fact, I carry *two* iPods with *identical* music programmed on both—in case of battery failure, loss, or any other tragic circumstance.

Music truly is my lifeline, marking time from the past to the present. Song after song after song creates an audio scrapbook of all my highs and lows. Music has always been there for me, on good days and bad.

And boy, did I ever need music in 2007. My iPod was like an IV drip.

Only now, when I look back, can I say the year 2007 was a gift. That's the year my body and my heart broke at the same time. You've probably had years like that—where even one of the challenges you face could drive you to your knees. But two? Again, only now can I see that two crises were actually a blessing, because I couldn't focus too long on one or the other.

The gift, disguised as a double sucker punch, unfolded like this: you know those movies when the people on screen are in the middle of a picnic or birthday party or something happy—and suddenly, out of nowhere, the freaky bogeyman sneaks up and whacks them in the back of the head with a two-by-four? That's kind of what happened to me.

I was forty-two years old, enjoying the wonderful movie picnic that was my life: comfortable in my job as a correspondent for *Dateline*, host of a television show called (ironically) *Your Total Health*, and newly married to the wonderful man I met and fell in love with in New Orleans. We had tied the knot in December of 2005, the Caribbean Sea painting a picture-perfect watercolor of our wedding. Family and friends joined us in tropical Punta Cana, a sultry province on the eastern tip of the Dominican Republic. The area is surreal, with its turquoise waters and gentle breezes. Even the Punta Cana

International Airport looks like a movie set, complete with beautifully crafted thatched huts for terminals. When our guests deplaned
into 80-degree temperatures, they were immediately greeted by steel
drum bands, the musicians dressed in colorful island garb.

Days before the wedding, my fiancé and I frolicked in the warm
sea, relaxed and enjoyed the ongoing arrival of each family member and friend. Resort staff was busy setting up the large, open-air
thatched hut that would house our reception. The color scheme was
fresh white sand and coconut brown, with accents of natural shells
and flickering candles. Everything reflected casual elegance. For the
ceremony, we chose the end of a small pier to say our vows, soft waves
lapping the wooden posts. The resort staff was limited, so we often
saw the same person serving in different roles. Remember how in
comedy shows, the judge would slip off his wig and put on a sheriff's
hat, then pop on the mayor's cap, then the milkman lid? That's how it
was there. I think the guy who took our bags married us. Who cared?!
It all unfolded exactly the way we'd hoped. A golf cart delivered me
to the marital pier. (I think the guy who made us fruity drinks was
also the guy who drove the cart.) Hala was my maid of honor, dressed
in a striking red satin dress. Adel walked me down the "aisle." All of
our guests gathered round in the sand as the sun set over the calm,
endless ocean. I'd never been married before and was forty-one years
old. The man I'd dated on and off for twelve years now became my
husband. We shared the dream of a life together and a family. I've always wanted kids and he did, too. I had finally balanced my personal
life and career, a real challenge for me up to this point.

One year later, we were living in a comfortable New York City
apartment. In early December of 2006, we left home to celebrate
our first anniversary in the cozy Pocono Mountains. Just a few weeks
later, we enjoyed the holidays. Christmas was perfect—you could see

it in all the photos. My husband, me, his family, surrounded by gifts and smiling. But sadly, pictures can be deceiving. I had no idea that right then, at the time of those very photographs, my body was breaking down—and so was my young marriage.

Just a few days after that lovely Christmas, I had an appointment with my gynecologist. Maybe you don't mind it, but I hate going to the gyno. I just do. I had no idea how much I'd *really* hate it this time. During my appointment, Dr. Erin DuPree did a routine breast exam. As her fingertips gently pushed and probed, she found a tiny lump in my left breast. Hmm. She pointed it out to me. It was pea-size. Maybe even smaller. (I'll be honest. I couldn't feel it. It's not like breasts are made of Jell-O and you can easily feel a marble in there. They're lumpy and bumpy. At least mine are.) Anyway, she asked me to have it checked out. So, I went in for a mammogram (my first ever), then an ultrasound, then a biopsy. All of these, all at once. All the makings of a starting line to a very long race.

The Biopsy

Would you like one lump or two? I would like neither, please. Turns out, I had two lumps. Two lumpy squatters that had been setting up camp inside me for who knows how long. Now, it was time to explore. Time to determine their intentions with the tip of a curious needle. The doctor described the biopsy as a way to remove tissue samples from the suspicious lumps in my breast. A pathologist would then study the samples for signs of trouble.

As I sat in the waiting room, I began searching for signs of trouble, too—in my marriage. My friend Karen was with me and both of our laps were covered with papers. I'd brought along two months of cell phone bills and also my calendar. Months earlier, I happened upon an inappropriate text message on my husband's cell phone. He claimed it was harmless and that the woman was an old friend. But in recent days, I'd noticed the same number on a phone bill I was paying. Disgusted and confused, I asked Karen to help me scour the cell phone records. The plan was to highlight calls and texts to a particular area code. We'd then cross-reference those dates with the days on my calendar when I was out of town. Talk about your shitty afternoons—waiting to get stuck in the boob with a needle and through the heart with a knife. Blanketed in printouts, I scanned for numbers until the nurse called my name for the procedure.

Being the woman in wait for the results of a breast biopsy is downright terrifying. I was numb. But somewhere, under all the numbness was terror, tingling below my skin, waiting to rush in like blood that flows back into an arm that's fallen asleep. I began to use a journal to tap off some of the fear that was pooling inside me. It overflowed from my brain, down into my pen, and onto these pages.

PAPER JOURNAL
JANUARY 27, 2007
SATURDAY

For the biopsy, I went into a room and they gave me local anesthesia. They flipped me around on the bed so I would be positioned just right. At *that* point, in that room with the dingy walls and that curtain, the sheet over me and the machine showing me exactly where those two lumps were—right at that moment—I got scared. The doc made a small incision and started poking around in there trying to get a piece of each lump. Pushing and poking. It seemed so aggressive the way the doctor pushed that probe around. It was like a bow and arrow. I watched the screen as he shot that arrow into the lump. I heard a *thunk* sound. I hoped it wasn't the sound of cancer.

CANCER. CANCER. CANCER. CANCER. Hmmm. When you write it four times in ALL CAPS it doesn't seem as scary. Look at it. I don't know why.

January has been an awful month. I found out my husband is deceiving me and now this. So twisted. The whole thing. Who would have thought one month could be so unhinging? When did it get like this? What if it is cancer? There is a big cry stuck in my throat waiting to be unleashed.

JANUARY 28 (DAY BEFORE DIAGNOSIS)
SUNDAY

Don't want to write much today. Good news: Hala came to visit. Bad news (which I hope turns into good news): I get results back tomorrow. Today I am cancer-free in my mind. I hope it is confirmed in my body. I am kind of nervous, but it has been nice having Hala here. She cooked Cornish hens and veggies tonight and we watched movies.

I am going to sleep now so I don't obsess.

Sleep that night was virtually impossible. I had two life-changing events happening at the exact same time. My marriage was a lie and I possibly had breast cancer. That January, I thought I would drown in grief. But, thankfully, a weird internal game plan kicked in. I guess in the name of survival, human beings must only be able to generate a finite amount of grief. Since I had two tragedies flooding my life at once, I instinctively began to "part" all of that grief—to split the raging sea of crap. When I was obsessing about my poisoned marriage, I'd immediately say to myself, *I pray to God it's not cancer*. When I was obsessing about my health, I'd think, *How in the hell can my marriage be over?* This kept me from getting too depressed about one or the other. It's almost like having two kids instead of one. You don't focus too much on the one who's screaming because the other one is coloring on the walls with your lipstick.

The Diagnosis

You should know, I'm an apple-eating, Central Park–running, early-to-bed healthy woman. *I thought* I was doing everything right, living right. But life is funny, isn't it? On Sunday, everything is perfectly normal. Then Monday comes and it all turns upside down. Monday is when I found out my lumps were bad actors. Malcontents. Badasses. I was in such shock that it took me until Tuesday to actually write down the C-word.

PAPER JOURNAL
JANUARY 30
TUESDAY

Okay—I have *CANCER*. That's what Dr. Kwai said. At 11 A.M. yesterday, I was talking to an intern in my office when my cell phone rang. It said Mount Sinai and I froze. The intern looked at me and I asked her to leave. But first, she asked if she could hug me.

Dr. Kwai said, "I have some not favorable news for you—the cells are cancerous." I asked, "Both lumps?" He said, "Yes." What in the hell is happening? *CANCER*??

Dr. Andrew Kwai told me I needed to have an MRI in the next few days for a closer look at my cancer. In shock, my brain defaulted to work and I asked him if it would be okay if I flew to Boston tomorrow to cover a story. He said, "Why not?"

Why not, Hoda? Because, my dear, you are *nuts right now* and have a lot of nerve thinking you can focus on work. I called Hala, and she met me at Dr. Christina Weltz's office, where we would learn about my biopsy results. "If you're going to have cancer," Dr. Weltz said, "this is the good one to get."

Good cancer? (Who knew?)

I felt such a lack of control! Let's put it this way: if they had done an MRI on my brain, it would have revealed a scorched matrix of question marks, exclamation points, and expletives. #@$%&#%! It was at this point that I began to write the word FORWARD a lot in my journal. A word that gave me a kernel of power, a tiny seed of control.

FORWARD.

I woke up the next day and headed to Boston to do a story for the *Today* show on "Rocker Moms"—older women who were slammin' on their electric guitars and rocking tight leather pants. The whole experience was out-of-body for me. For them, it was a chance to tell me all about their music and their lives. They were so excited. I was so out of it. One minute I was laughing hysterically, the next I was just watching their lips move in slow motion.

Do I really have cancer? the floating me wondered.

The following day, I was back in New York for my MRI. I needed one to help doctors determine how they would rid me of the cancer. Was there cancer between the lumps? Could they just take the lumps or would I need a mastectomy and breast reconstruction? The whole experience was aggravating. Hala came with me and stayed, even as I was placed inside the tube. I was terrified because of what the MRI might reveal, not to mention my loathing of the tube-o'-claustrophobia. Right before the procedure, the technician told Hala she had to leave the room.

"The waves the machine sends out are not safe for you," he explained.

My sister, as always, did not skip a beat in her protection of me. She pulled up a chair, sat down, and said, "I'm not leaving."

The machine cranked up and drummed "Rat-a-tat-tat . . . tat-tat-tat" for a solid forty minutes. I felt rat-a-tat-rattled. So many forms to fill out, questions, a dye injection, the tube, more forms. Finally, we bolted out of there and I headed to work. I had to tape two *Your Total Health* shows for NBC. Getting my makeup done and hair blown out felt ridiculous. Trying to make pretty out of such an ugly situation. I got into the studio and we began taping. As I read the teleprompter, every story seemed to be about a devastating illness. I was reading the words and once again floating above it all, wondering whose life I was watching.

"We'll be right back with a woman and her sister's battle with cancer," I read as we rolled tape.

"Hoda," a producer said, "Can you do that again? We had a glitch with the camera."

"We'll be right back with a woman and her sister's battle with cancer."

"Hoda, just one more time. Sorry."

I wanted to scream.

Finally, the taping was over. I went back to my office and saw the red light on my desk phone blinking. I knew it was the results of the MRI. "Hoda," the message said, "the results of the MRI are incomplete. Please call us." When I finally reached the doctor, he told me the two cancerous lumps were farther apart than they originally thought, but that there was no cancer, thankfully, in between them. *But* they found another lump in the same breast.

God. More anxiety. More #@$%&#%!

February 2007

All of the doctors said the same thing: I needed a mastectomy, no choice. Three lumps, spread out—they could not save the breast. No more breast? We have to annihilate my left breast?

One doctor asked, "Do you identify with your breasts?"

Huh?

"How attached *are* you to your breasts?"

"Well . . . I *like* 'em. I mean, if you showed me twenty breasts in a lineup, I *think* I would be able to pick mine out." (I think they're *those* . . . but they mayyy beee thoossse . . .)

This seems like a good time to talk about my video journal. After all, there are some things—like your breasts—that you only want to ruminate about with yourself. The video journal was the brainchild of *Your Total Health* executive producer Betsy Wagner. She offered a smart approach when she found out about my diagnosis: "At least give yourself a choice. You can decide later whether you want to air any of it." She gave me a home video camera and told me to record as much or as little as I wanted, whenever I wanted. We thought perhaps the videos could one day help our *Your Total Health* viewers. Ironically, that camera turned out to be a good way for me to vent without having to burden anyone.

VIDEO JOURNAL
ONE WEEK BEFORE SURGERY
(IN MY BEDROOM, LYING ON THE BED)

"What woman has really stared at her breasts long enough to know what they look like? I know I haven't. So, most of the time during the day, I forget I have breast cancer. I just forget— because I lived forty-two years and some months without it. I lived most of my life without it, so that's why it makes sense that just like that *(I snap my fingers)*, everything changes.

"Last month, I forgot that I have breast cancer. And then one guy made a chemo joke, like, 'Oh, that guy looks so bald, looks like he had chemo.' They were talking about someone on *American Idol*. And I immediately got this, like twitch. (I twitch my eye.) I have a weird way I deal with things, and I remember this from when I went to Afghanistan or Iraq. I just don't think anything bad is going to happen to me. Just like that. I really don't. I think I can go into a dangerous place, or be put into a dangerous situation, and for some reason, nothing will happen to me. Now, maybe that's arrogant or ego. I really hope it's not. But I really don't think about it—I just don't obsess about it."

Why obsess? There was nothing I could do. My left breast had to go.

It took me about a month to find the right doctor and hospital. The scary surgery was only a few weeks away. And that's when I had my dream. Have you ever had a dream that is *so* vivid you're *sure* it's true? In my dream, I was lying in bed and the doctors were surrounding me. They said, "Hoda, we are *so* sorry. We made a mistake." It felt so *real*. I believed it. The doctors were wrong. I *knew* it! But when I woke up, I pulled down my T-shirt and there they were. Three black X's—marks the doctor had made on my chest to identify the location of the lumps. Damn the luck! It was all *too* real.

Those weeks leading up to my surgery felt surreal. Like I was living someone else's life. I remember flying to London for work, listening to the Jo Dee Messina song "Was That My Life" over and over again. I'd been diagnosed on paper, but my brain had not yet gotten the memo. Very little was getting through to me despite the very big effort made by others. Thoughtful people were plying me with dozens of books about surviving breast cancer and getting healthy, but only one made an impression. One I had bought for myself. In *Meditations*, Marcus Aurelius writes, "Think of yourself as dead. You have lived your life. Now, take what's left and live it properly." I liked that. Stop wasting time. Unfortunately and unavoidably, most of my time during those weeks was eaten up by consultations with doctors, delivering work speeches, and meeting with my divorce attorney. I was sick—physically and emotionally. I tried to focus on what my *Dateline* boss, David Corvo, told me. He said, "Hoda, all the women I know who've had breast cancer have one thing in common: they're still here."

March Begins

The first few days of March, NBC asked me to shoot a pilot for a morning show tentatively called *Fresh Squeezed*. My coanchor was Touré, an author, TV personality, and contributing writer for *Rolling Stone* magazine. We had fun and the project was a good distraction. When that ended, I knew I had just one thing left to focus on: my surgery.

VIDEO JOURNAL
MARCH 1
(IN MY OFFICE AT NBC)

"The good thing about focusing on this (I roll out a poster for *Fresh Squeezed*), is I'm not focusing on the bigger thing. And the bigger thing is, I'm having surgery on . . . Tuesday? Listen to me . . . like I don't remember. Of course I remember. It's Tuesday. Tuesday's the day.

"But I'm weird about big things. Sometimes with big things, I table them. I don't think about them. I've only had three big moments in my life. And every time, I'm just sort of, I'm out.

"There was one time in Burma. We were lying in a canoe, it was nighttime and rebel soldiers were paddling the canoe. And if we got caught, we were going to jail for seven years. And I'll tell you one thing, I was Steady Eddie. I was calm because you know what, I was out, I was completely out.

"We were in Baghdad, they were shooting bombs all around us, it was like, bang-bang-bang! and you know what? I was completely out. I felt completely calm.

"And that's what I feel on this one, with the surgery. I'm out, like what can I possibly do? Seriously? I can't study up on it, because what does it matter what I study? The more I read, the more freaked I get. I keep praying to God that my doctor gets good rest, she sleeps well, has a good dinner, wakes up bright-eyed and bushy-tailed, and does the surgery . . . because there's not really a thing I can do.

"The weird thing about me is, I'm a control freak. I'm a control freak about everything, except when I'm completely out, which is what I am about this surgery. I'm out."

Sometimes I just wanted to be alone with the camera or completely alone, but mostly, I was grateful for the company of my sister. Thank God for Hala. She had swooped in like a mother bird to protect me the minute I was diagnosed.

PAPER JOURNAL
MARCH 2

The pregame has been easier than I thought, thanks to one person. Hala. She has been a godsend and I will be forever in her debt. She has been an incredible support. She keeps my mind off everything bad. We laugh at home, she cooks great meals, we talk, I don't focus on surgery or my marriage, and that's the key. I don't know what I would have done without her.

On March 5, the day before my surgery, my mom flew in. I could tell she was worried. She was thinner and there was a lot of arguing—fear's disguise. Still, I was so glad she was there.

PAPER JOURNAL
MARCH 5 (DAY BEFORE SURGERY)

I feel strangely calm. There's not a single thing I can do about this. I love this feeling of surrender. Today I will go to the park, get my hair done, then go to the hospital for pre-op stuff. I don't know what to expect, but the nurse said, "You'll feel like you got hit by a Mack truck." That's never happened to me so I don't know what that feels like, but I imagine it's not pleasant. I don't want to delve too deeply here because I'm afraid I'll get scared, and who wants that? More later—off to the park for a run.

My surgery was scheduled for two o'clock, but I had to be at the hospital by noon. The three of us spent the morning together trying to relax. It was one of those almost artificial mornings. No one wanted to pet the giant elephant in the room.

"Okay, is everyone ready? Did we pack the Oil of Olay skin cream?"

We were talking about ridiculous things, because what else are you going to talk about?

VIDEO JOURNAL
DAY OF SURGERY
(IN MY BEDROOM)

"They said I'm supposed to go into surgery at two o'clock. It's supposed to be an eight-hour procedure, and they'll cut out the cancer in the breast, and then they move belly fat up into the breast area.

"Nasty, nasty to think about. *(I laugh.)* In fact, when the doctors try to tell me details, I go, yeah yeah yeah, yeah. Yeah, go. Just do it, you do it. I just want to come out with bandages on. I'm not one who loves to know, ' . . . and then we're going to take your belly fat and tunnel it up into your breast area and fuse . . .' I was like this: blah-blah-blah. *(I shiver.)* Ugh. I just don't like to hear it. So anyway, they're going to do what they have to do, I'm going to lie there, I'm going to wake up, I'm going to take morphine, drip-drip-drip-drip, and hopefully just heal and everything will be better.

"I mean I think I'll be five days in the hospital, so it's not going to be simple, obviously. I don't know, it's weird. It's like when you've never ever been through something and people ask, 'What do you think it's going to be like?' I've never been cut at all, I've never been under anesthesia at all, so I don't know. But I feel *okay* right this second.

"I'm thinking when you don't know what to expect, you expect the worst . . . like someone is sawing you, or the recovery's going to feel like this . . . or post-op will be like that. I've kind of almost avoided talking to people who have had this, and I don't know if it's a smart thing or not. But, a lot of people are saying to me, 'Hey, call me—I'll tell you. I did this, I did that . . .' But, sometimes you know, some people just . . . they make you more scared. Because my mom and my sister are here and they're completely hilarious, it's just been fun. We're doing stupid things, watching *American Idol,* reading the paper, you know, they're both cooking."

(I WALK OUT OF THE BEDROOM WITH THE CAMERA ROLLING AND HEAD TOWARD MY KITCHEN AREA)

"Oh, hold on, come here, there's something I need to show you . . . let me tell you what we've been doing."

(I WALK INTO THE KITCHEN)

"This is very important . . . what I'm about to reveal on the videotape.

"Where are the Mega Millions tickets? Wait, let's see.

"My sister has hidden her Mega Millions tickets, which we just bought today. Here they are."

(HALA LAUGHS)

"Twenty dollars, is that what you got? Twenty bucks' worth. Were they quick picks? Because Hala is very lucky and so is my mother, who is hiding under the cabinet. And Hala is very lucky. And I'm usually—when it comes to lotteries and jackpots—not. So I'm using *The Secret,* Oprah's pick, and I'm welcoming all good things. So what's the jackpot again?"

HALA: I don't know, three hundred and some . . .

ME: Three hundred and three hundred fifty-five, so when I come out of the surgery, we'll have four hundred million dollars to spend, and don't reveal where we're hiding our Mega Millions tickets.

HALA: Don't show anything.

ME: When's the drawing? Tonight?

HALA: Tonight.

ME: What time? Ten? Eleven?

HALA: When you come out of surgery.

ME: I come out of surgery and then we win the Mega Millions.

HALA: That's right.

MOM: But we won't find out until tomorrow.

ME: We won't find out until tomorrow. But they'll have a TV in the hospital.

MOM: But we can't take them with us.

ME: Yeah, we can't take them with us. Nobody take the Mega Millions. Leave them here. We have our priorities set.

HALA: Yeah, surgery? What surgery? We're thinking ahead to the . . .

ME: Yes, the spending of the Mega Millions.

Late morning, my mom, Hala, and I took the subway to Columbia University Medical Center and had some good laughs en route. A few blocks from CUMC, we walked by a street cart filled with falafel balls and all the spicy sauces. Man, did that smell good! I was not allowed to eat since the day before, so I was starving. Once inside, staff began to prepare me for surgery. *Dateline* and *Your Total Health* producer Katherine Chan was in the room shooting video with a hand-held camera. Weird. A video starring my breast.

Once I was prepped, my plastic surgeon, Dr. Jeffrey Ascherman, came into the room. He asked me to remove my gown and began drawing on me with a magic marker. (If only that marker *was* magic, right?) With purple ink, he drew a shape—sort of like an eye—on my belly. I assumed that was targeted for removal, as the plan was to use my belly fat to reconstruct my breast. He drew dotted lines down the center of my chest and across my hips. I was a human blueprint, about to be reconstructed. I kept looking at my body—this body—*one last time.*

Next, my surgeon appeared—Dr. Freya Schnabel. She held my hand and told me everything would be fine. When my mom saw Freya, she started bawling. This woman would have the fate of her daughter in those hands. They were the first tears I'd seen from my mom since she arrived. Seeing my mom cry made Hala cry. The doctor reassured them both she would take very good care of me.

On to the operating room—cold and stark. I climbed up onto the table, where nurses wrapped my legs in something, then covered me with a blanket that blew out puffs of warm air. I looked up at the bright light overhead and got scared. That's when I really got scared.

Dr. Schnabel took my hand again. "This is the flurry of activity I was telling you about before we operate. Don't worry," she said calmly. "Everything will be fine."

Something covered my mouth and I began to relax. I was told the surgery would take about eight hours. My mom and Hala were waiting outside.

The surgery to remove the cancer took about two hours. It was the reconstruction that ate up the next 360 minutes. I remember waking up to the anesthesiologist telling me I was okay. Groggy and doped up, I slowly realized I was in the recovery room. My mom and Hala came in to say hello, but looking back, it's still pretty fuzzy. When they rolled me into my hospital room, the nurse told me I had to move from the gurney to the bed.

"It's easy," she said, "Go shoulder to shoulder, hip to hip, then inch your way over."

I was still high as a kite from the anesthesia, so I did it and didn't feel a thing. Sleeping was harder. I just couldn't do it. People were checking on me constantly, which is a good thing, but not for sleeping. Somewhere in the early-morning hours, a nurse came in and said she wanted to clean me up a bit. She helped me get up from the bed and walk to a table. I saw spots and felt nauseated. Everyone around me was telling me how good I was doing, cheering me on.

"Look at you! You're in the top three percent when it comes to postsurgery recovery time!"

Barf. Drains in my breast, a catheter. Everything was coming out of my body. This was all a shock to me, considering I'd never had surgery before. Not for tonsils, not for wisdom teeth, no broken bones, nothing. My body was officially jumping into the deep end with no swimming lessons. You know my morphine button got a workout.

"Tap . . . tap . . . tap-tap-tap."

At one point, I pressed the button and nothing came out. I thought it was broken, but the nurse explained that it would only administer morphine every six minutes. I'd been asking for it at four. The medicine made me feel awful, but it did relieve the pain.

"Tap . . . tap."

I was mostly out of it as people came by to visit. Fuzzy, fuzzy, and fuzzier. At one point, I felt so overwhelmed that I asked everyone to please leave the room. I asked for a sleeping pill, too. I needed to rest my mind. I woke up the next day wanting to stretch, like any normal morning. Bad idea.

Post op with Mom

VIDEO JOURNAL
DAY AFTER SURGERY
(LYING IN MY HOSPITAL BED)

"It's the day after. It's been, uh, how long . . . two-thirty now . . . so I was out of surgery last night. I think I was kind of remembering where I was about midnight. So today's the pain day. It's the day where you feel like—I mean they kept saying you'll feel like you got hit by a Mack truck, and of course, I didn't know what that felt like until today—and now I do.

"They say the cut across my abdomen is twice as long as a C-section. And then there's the cut where they took the entire breast out. And then they moved everything up. So, I feel kind of groggy, just out of it and, um—you know, I stood up today, which was a big deal, and walked over to that table over there and had breakfast. Came back, sat down, and I think the lady's going to come back today and walk me around, which I'm dreading. The idea of walking, just the idea of getting up. Think about it—if you have an incision hip to hip, I'm not trying to complain or whine, but you've gotta swivel your hips to even hoist yourself up—you can't lean, you can't do anything.

"This is the worst pain I've ever felt. I mean, I haven't given birth so I don't know what that feels like, but this is pretty crummy. And this here is the magic button—it's the morphine drip. You see? *(I press the button and the machine beep-beeps)* When you hear those two beeps—beep-beep—I think it's going into me somewhere . . . I don't know where it's going . . . I think it's maybe that IV. Who cares? It's in there. You're supposed to use it as often as you want but it regulates, so if I continue to push it as I want to, it won't give me anything. Bastard.

"They said it went really well. I mean they were all talking about how the first part of the surgery took an hour and a half, and that was good. They said it was supposed to take longer. And the guy was really proud of his reconstruction . . . he kept saying how quickly it went and that was great. I mean it wasn't quick—it took freakin' eight hours—but to him I guess it was. He said they took out all the belly fat they could find, I guess, and moved it up. He said that it was tight in there. It's so tight. It's how it feels now. It's so tight you can't stand up fully. You're supposed to sit hunched over until it pulls. It's almost like getting a nip-tuck in your stomach, which is the fringe benefit of this surgery. But they have to have enough fat to put in your breast, so that's a lot, so they're digging around trying to find it.

"Dr. Ascherman gave me a big gold star for the surgery. He kept saying because I'm healthy, I think, aside from the cancer, because I'm a healthy person, I think, in terms of exercise and eating right, it was easier for them to do the surgery. I guess that made it less difficult, less painful. I'm so glad it's over. I am *so* glad it's over. I mean, I feel like shit right now and everything, I feel terrible, but I am glad it is over, it is out of me, it is over. And that's probably the main thing I'm feeling, just relieved that it's over. And then you know, there's always the next phase about the pathology and what is that going to do, and who knows? But I'm not even caring about that right now. I just want to stand up and walk around, do the little things.

"They took out a big clump of lymph nodes, six of them, and checked them. So I don't know when they come back with the results. I haven't seen the doctor today. I think we'll know in a few days.

"I cannot believe I was running in Central Park yesterday. It's weird. One day you're in Central Park; the next day you're laid out."

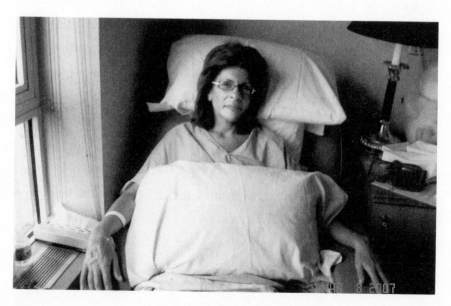

Where's the morphine?!

All the routine things, like sitting up and getting up to go to the bathroom, were a struggle. A nurse helped me into the bathroom, and there it was—the mirror. Slowly, I took off my gown and looked. Horrors. My left breast had a 6-by-4-inch chunk of skin on it from my stomach. The patch was darker and out of place, because it was tanned from a recent trip to Puerto Rico with my mom. That just added to the freakish image of it all. I felt like one of those pictures I'd seen in the breast cancer books. Bizarre. I turned away from the mirror. The nurse said, "Baby, we got to wash you." I said, "Can you wash me facing *this* way?"

I could not look at my breast. I don't know what I was expecting. But it was horrifying to me. I was disfigured.

The nurse asked, "Well, are you sure? It's easier for me to wash you if you face the mirror."

"No," I said. "This is easier for me. Trust me. This is better."

As she began to clean me up, I remember thinking, *Who was that in the mirror?*

Dr. Ascherman came into the bathroom and talked about how good his work looked. Really? I wished it was already healed.

Several days and zero showers later, I was released from the hospital. By now, you know right where I headed first.

Yep—to get my hair blown out!

I took my hospital pillow with me and got just the medicine I needed after my surgery. Now it was time to recover and to research the next step. Did I need radiation? Chemotherapy? The yes or no decision after the hip-to-hip incision.

PAPER JOURNAL
MARCH 22
9 P.M.

Today was not a good day. I went to one of the best breast cancer oncologists, and he said that (1) I need chemo, and (2) I'll never have kids. My God, it was jarring. He was glib and arrogant. I will never go back to him.

Elizabeth Edwards had a news conference today to say her cancer had come back. She got breast cancer again—in her bones. She *did* chemo and it came back. The odds apparently for me are 3 to 4 percent better if I do the chemo—that's it. So is 3 to 4 percent worth it? When Elizabeth Edwards did chemo and it *still* came back? Tough call.

Two more oncologists and then I'll see. I'm leaning toward *no* right now. My cancer is supposedly the kind that doesn't even respond well to chemo. It's all so confusing.

The good news was, the surgery removed all the cancer, and pathology reports indicated that my lymph nodes were clear. *Huge* news. The confusing news was, I got three different opinions from three different oncologists on whether or not I should get chemotherapy.

One doctor said I *must* have chemo. "It's imperative."

One doctor said I didn't need to have chemo. "Just take the pills."

The third doctor said I couldn't make a mistake either way. "It's a personal decision."

So, I had three of the top oncologists giving me three different opinions. It was a bit unnerving. I was sitting there thinking, *Wow. You'd think all these guys would look at the same results and have the same answer.*

But they didn't.

After several more meetings, I decided the best choice for me was tamoxifen. It's a little pill with big consequences, especially for someone my age, on the tail end of my childbearing years. Tamoxifen basically makes your body uninhabitable for a baby—poison. For about five years. So, by choosing to take it, I also lost a choice about my future. Cruel, but I'm alive, so I can't complain. I'll bet you've had to make some crappy decisions in your life, too.

VIDEO JOURNAL
THREE WEEKS AFTER SURGERY
(LYING ON MY BED)

"I'm forty-two and they're telling me I can't have kids and I don't even want to think about that. And then my whole relationship, my marriage. I've been trying to say in my head I have two cancers, and I'm getting rid of both of them. It sounds harsh, but you've got to look at things like that sometimes. I'm done. I'm done with it. I'm done with the marriage. I'm done."

Is there ever a "good" time for a divorce? I don't know. Maybe. For me, the timing was brutal. In the same week, I was diagnosed with breast cancer *and* found out there were serious issues in my marriage. My broken breast was located directly over my broken heart, and managing both was excruciating. I probably deceived myself by walking down the aisle. Despite all I knew going in, I was sure our marriage would work. I was wrong. Since then, my breast and my heart have been reconstructed—both are still a work in progress. I met my former husband on Valentine's Day, 1994. Our divorce was final exactly fourteen years later, Valentine's Day, 2008.

In the spirit of a tell-all book, I will tell all who've been through or are going through a divorce this:

1. You will never regret taking the high road, as hard as it may be to do. Your dignity and class are to be treasured—try to maintain both.

2. Share all your dirty details with very few. Understand that the reasons behind sharing all the details are not always smart. People should not be expected to take sides. This was your marriage and you were both responsible for its care and feeding. Bad decisions may certainly have been made, but broadcasting details everywhere is not of value.

3. Take things one day at a time. Try not to look too far ahead. There is nothing productive about wishing the time forward, to a place you can't control. Do a good job each day and expect bad days, too.

4. Manage your money well. Do not medicate with money unless you have lots to spare. Save for a rainy day because, as you've found out, there are unexpected downpours.

5. Take care of yourself. Be healthy and wise and don't forget to smile. It feels like the world has ended, but each day is still a gift. Do your best to feel grateful for all you still have.

6. Give yourself a year to feel at least close to normal again. Create a good "new" normal. You are in charge of the tone of your world. Make it a happy one.

7. Don't forget to thank all the people who love, support, and help you. And be aware that they can never feel the depth of your pain, just as you can't know theirs. They are simply doing their best to shine light on your darkest days. (And don't take advantage of their battery power—help yourself, too.)

8. Don't ever Google your ex. Sure, a part of you would love to see a photo of him holding a "Will Work for Food" sign, but move on. Your job is to move forward, not waste time double-clicking on your past.

9. Do something for someone else. Our burdens feel lighter when we help carry someone else's for a day or even an hour.

10. Forgive. It will make you stronger and lighter. We don't have to forget, but to forgive is freeing.

13

MAN ON THE PLANE

In the weeks following my surgery, I didn't write in my journal. I couldn't. My arm was in a sling to prevent blood clots and my body was in healing mode. Everything was tender. Looking back, I probably decided too early to travel again for the *Today* show.

In May of 2007, just two months after my surgery, I agreed to fly to Ireland to shoot a "Where in the World Is Matt Lauer?" segment in Galway. We arrived in Ireland, the shoot went well, and I boarded my flight back home to New York. I hunkered down in my seat, tried to relax, and hoped I would get some sleep. My plan was to listen to music and tune out. Boy, am I glad I didn't strap on my iPod five minutes earlier. I would have missed one of the most important moments of my life.

Just as I was fiddling around for my ear plugs, a stranger sitting in the seat next to me said hello. I was tired and sore, but politely said hi back. We exchanged pleasantries and chatted for a while. Then he asked me in a heavy Boston accent, "What's the knock on ya at work?"

"Huh?"

"What is the knock on ya at work? What do your bosses say when ya walk out of the room? Everyone has one. What's yours? Like, why aren't ya Katie or Meredith?"

Hmm.

Funny thing is, I was not offended. There was something likable about this guy. So I answered. "Well," I said. "I fill in a lot on the *Today* show, so I kind of feel like a guest in the house. Like it's not my house. I don't volunteer a lot of information about myself on the air. I wait to be asked."

He said, "Here's some advice: people don't ask."

"Okay, so what's the knock on *you* at your work?"

"I'm ugly and I'm not very smart. But I read people well and that's why I'm a good VP at my company."

We made more small talk about our lives, then he asked me what was on my arm. I was wearing a medical sleeve to prevent blood clots on the plane. With a bunch of lymph nodes taken out, you have to help keep your blood circulating. I said it was a compression sleeve. He asked what it was for.

I said, "I had a procedure and the docs want me to wear it."

"What *kind* of procedure?"

I said I had an *operation*.

"What *kind* of operation?" he persisted.

(I still liked him.)

Finally, I said, "Okay, I'll tell you. I have breast cancer. But I hope when you get off this plane you don't say, 'Hey, I sat next to a woman with breast cancer.' I hope you have four or five other things you think of *before* breast cancer."

He said, "What is wrong with you? Breast cancer is a part of you.

Like going to college, working at NBC, getting married. I'm going to give you some advice," he said. "And then I'll let you go to sleep."

Okay.

He said the following words, which mean so much to me today: "Don't hog your journey. It's not just for *you*. Think of how many people you could have helped on the plane ride home." He went on: "You can take your business, shove it deep in your pockets, and take it to your grave. Or you can help someone. It's your choice."

Right then, I made my choice, a decision I'd been wrestling with for quite a while.

14

THE GAME CHANGER

As you may know, October is National Breast Cancer Awareness month. Since my own diagnosis was in late January 2007, I had a few months to decide whether or not I wanted to share my experience with *Today* show viewers during that special month. With zero pressure and 100 percent support, Ann Curry asked me one day if I'd thought about sharing my story of being a breast cancer survivor. It felt odd. Typically, I was the one asking someone if they'd like to tell *me* their story. Now here I was—the decision to come forward and talk about myself resting in my lap. I told her I'd think about it. I trusted Ann to handle the experience with kid gloves, and I felt completely comfortable with her kind spirit. I just wasn't sure I wanted to make something that was so private so public.

Then came that darn guy on the plane. Talking about deep pockets, taking stuff to my grave, sharing my journey. I knew I had to do it. I wanted to do it. I went to Ann and told her I was in. I knew I'd have some control over what I wanted included or left out. But—*surprise!* Turns out I was as tender as my fresh incision. I was much more vulnerable than I'd thought. When Ann and I sat down on that couch and the cameras started rolling, for the first time I *really* understood what it's like to be on the other side of the interview—the person in the hot seat, praying to God that the interviewer will take good care of her story. The videotape began to capture our interview.

ANN (softly): Are you mourning the loss of your old self?

I instantly thought, *What?!* She was asking me questions *out loud* that I was avoiding in my head. And I agreed to this? I remember thinking, *I should not be doing this. This is too soon.* But it was too late. There I was, putting my business out there. And not just public-figure business like "I have two dogs and sometimes they sleep under the covers with me." This was painful stuff, close to the heart.

ANN: So, you're mourning a couple of things. You're mourning the loss of what was your body.

ME: Yeah. Some days I'm in the shower and I'm like, *Jesus. My God. I'm so upset.* And some days I'm thinking, *Hold on a second. You got your life back. And if this is the scar that shows it, y'know, embrace it.*

ANN: You're mourning the fact that you, you know, how you're thinking who you once were, that sort of carefree girl is gone.

ME: Uh-huh. Yeah.

ANN: But on the other hand, you got something great back.

ME: Yes. I feel different. I feel better than I felt. I feel stronger than I felt.

ANN: Based on what the doctors are telling you, you'll never have children.

ME: Not have them—right.

ANN: Because of this.

ME: Right. I will not be able to have children that way because of this. And that's hard. I mean, I can't even—I can't even open that door. Like, I can't even go down that road. But, I keep thinking, you know, life is about options and choices. There will be other options. I'm sure there are a lot of . . . there's probably some child out there for me somewhere that needs me.

This videotaped interview ran as part of our *live* segment on the *Today* show in October for Breast Cancer Awareness month. There I was on the couch with Ann, *live* in studio with no chance to edit anything. We ran the taped segment we shot earlier, then came back out live to just the two of us. When the red lights lit atop the in-studio cameras, I almost instantly began blubbering. Barely in control of my tear ducts or my voice, I choked out the story of the man on the plane.

What was happening?

That couch was normally where I laughed and joked, but here I was *crying* with Ann on live TV! It was a hard couple of minutes. She handled the conversation beautifully and steered me in the right direction, while I was blinded by my own personal baggage flying around everywhere. Uncomfortable, naked, exposed—that's just not me. And the worst part was that everyone was looking at me with Poor You eyes. It was my own fault! By the end of the segment, I felt uneasy, but unbeknownst to (poor) me, something incredible was happening outside the studio walls. Within minutes, emails began to come in from women across the country:

I, too, am a breast cancer survivor. Thank you so much for telling us about yourself. Somehow hearing it from you makes me feel not quite so alone.

Pat

I was diagnosed with breast cancer in June. I am grateful to you for going public because I think you can be instrumental in finding the cure with your very public place on the *Today* show.

Nan

Thank you, thank you, thank you! I just finished watching your interview. You touched my heart and opened my eyes to the very real possibility of facing breast cancer. I am scheduling my very overdue mammogram this morning. You have helped more than you will ever know.

Karen

I celebrated my fifth year in remission this past August. I was diagnosed at age thirty-five—I'll be forty-one in November and happy and (cross my fingers) healthy. The biggest thing I've learned is to smash my own spiders and get on with my day. There will be another!

Patti

My mother is a two-time survivor of breast cancer, as is my sister-in-law. Despite this, I have been too busy to make my mammogram appointment—moving, changing jobs, etc. When I saw your segment, I jumped up off the couch and ran to the phone. Staying alive needs no excuse. Thank you, thank you, thank you.

Mary Jo

Thank you for sharing that young, seemingly healthy people can be struck by cancer. Many people think it is only a disease of older age and postmenopausal women. You will inspire many younger women to be screened, I am sure. Everyone always thinks there is a tomorrow and doesn't realize there may not be. Thank you also for sharing the personal details, as the disfigurement part of our disease is a huge part of the battle. Thank you for saying if they are the scars to be alive, then great! That's a new way of looking at all my scars when I just feel so ugly because of them. Best wishes!

Jane Doe

I do not have cancer and it is not in my family. But I am a survivor of rape, and today thanks to your words, I can go another day. You said that someone on a plane told you not to be selfish with your journey and I immediately started crying because my journey has been painful, at least I thought so before today. Thank you so much for sharing your journey, it gave me courage to share mine. Women survivors are a special breed. I love you for what you did today! God bless you.

Dionne

Thank you, Hoda! I'm thirty-nine and will schedule my first mammogram *today* because of *you*. You're so brave. Thank you. Thank you. Forward!!

Kristen

Thank you for making me cry . . . and making me feel
vulnerable for just those few moments. Those moments are
the ones that keep me aware and human!

Cindy

I celebrated my tenth year as a survivor. You have joined
a sorority that none of us wants to join; however, we are
connected for a lifetime. We are sisters, and our energy
helps to support those going through just as you have gone
through.

RJA

I was blown away by the generous and honest responses that
came flooding in. It hit me right then that telling my story on the
Today show was a game changer. Originally, I thought there would
be no next step. This would be the hard part—reliving my story—and
then I could recoil into relative privacy about it. I was *so* wrong. What
I thought was the end was actually the beginning. These incredible
emails were just the beginning of a "sisterhood," as RJA put it. And
the sisterhood has a huge family tree—with brothers, fathers, moth-
ers, boyfriends, girlfriends, and millions of other members who are
touched by breast cancer. On the streets of New York, people started
to grab me, hug me, and say, "June 5, 2000. That's when I found out
about mine." Or, "Hoda, my sister had it and you are going to be *fine*."

I was now the Girl with Breast Cancer.

I'll never forget, just two days after the *Today* show story aired, I
flew to Virginia to speak at a Virginia Tech fundraiser. As I was walking around talking to people, several older men came up to me and
said, "How ya doin'?" (Picture them all looking down at my boobs *as*
they were asking.)

I thought, *Don't you mean, "How are they doin'?"* Good Lord, this was a new phenomenon. I was like, "Up here, Poppie (two fingers V-ed at my eyes). Keep it up *here*."

Several weeks later, I was walking on the beach with my mom in Delaware when a guy walked right up and said, "Hey, Hoda, my wife had breast cancer, too! How you feelin'?"

That's just how it was going to be from now on. And it was okay with me.

I have to say, I do feel a bit undeserving of all the attention about it. I feel unworthy to say "I went through this" when *so* many people have gone through much more than I did. No radiation for me, no chemotherapy for me. I did not lose my hair, I have never (knock wood) relapsed. Countless survivors have had to survive so much more than I. All I can do is focus on the fact that perhaps I have a platform to do *something* about it.

And here's what I feel that something is: Look at me, see how healthy I am now. I was weak, but now I'm strong. Clearly, there are legions of women like me who've gone through what I have and *are* living stronger and better. But they don't have a platform. Maybe I can be their humble representative. My hope is that if someone is totally in the weeds, like I was, they can see there *is* a path out. If someone feels despair, I want them to feel hope that life *can* get better. I'm always grateful when someone stops me to say, "You look good. You look like you're having fun. I can't believe you had cancer." Let's make this clear—I don't fancy myself as some sort of Pink Pioneer. So many before me with bigger platforms have done the same thing. Brave survivors we all know made it infinitely easier for me to come forward. Olivia Newton-John, Jaclyn Smith, Linda Ellerbee, Sheryl Crow, Melissa Etheridge, Christina Applegate, and on and on and on. The days are long gone when breast cancer was viewed as a broken wing. Now it seems more of a reason to take flight and soar!

One of the questions I'm often asked by people now is, "How can I help someone I love who's battling breast cancer?"

My answer is this: "Don't look at 'em funny." You know what I'm talking about—the Look. For me, one of the worst emotions I can have directed my way is pity. Sad eyes. Eyes that say, "You're different. You're not you anymore. We've lost you." Yes, the Look is completely out of love, but if you're the Lookee, you can't help but think, *Holy crap—I must look really bad. This must be really bad!*

Hell, before this happened to me, I'm quite sure I shot a holster full of Looks, thinking I was helping. Now, I gently suggest to people that they treat their sick loved one like they always have. Just be there for them, and let them know they are still the same person you know and love dearly. Cancer may steal your breast, but it *cannot* steal you.

Most of the time, I don't think about my cancer experience. And that's good. But, because I am now the Girl with Breast Cancer, I'm never really too far from it. And that's good, too. If you forget about what happens in your life, you often go back to the way you used to live it. Like after someone dies and you say, "I'm going to be different now. I'm going to do *more* of this and *less* of that." But pretty soon, you're just you again. That will be harder for me to do and it will be harder for me to forget the lessons. I have an army of people reminding me all the time, "This is who you are now! And don't forget it!"

Don't get me wrong. I still struggle with some of it. There's nothing fun about a disfigured—albeit—reconstructed breast. It's uncomfortable for *me* to look at it sometimes, so imagine dating. You already have enough regular issues that come along with romance and now another one? God, now I have to explain *this* thing? Well, I see it this way: only the right guy gets to see my left breast.

15

GET IN THE GAME

One morning, about two months after my surgery, I headed for Central Park for a walk. I stopped at a traffic light right before the park and saw a stream of people flowing along the sidewalk. Thousands of people walking together. I thought, *Oh, man, this whole mob of people. I better wait.* As I stood on the corner, I began to notice the pink. T-shirts, sneakers, hats. I could tell some of the women were recovering from breast cancer treatment because they were bald. Others were holding photographs of loved ones they'd lost. I hadn't remembered that this was the day of the 5K Revlon Run/Walk for Women. I watched all the participants go by and I began to clap.

"Clap, clap, clap . . . watch, watch, watch."

Then I started to cry. Tears began to stream down my face as I clapped. These were my sisters, and I was standing on the sidelines. I stood there like an outsider when I was actually totally connected to them and their—our—cause. They didn't know.

I decided it was time to get in the game. Time to stop clapping and start changing my attitude about my cancer experience. I wanted so badly to put it behind me that I'd denied the need to keep it in the forefront, too. To support and be supported by others. I watched until the very last person walked past. Instead of entering the park, I turned around and walked back home. I was tired and rejuvenated at the same time. The man on the plane, deciding to share my story on the *Today* show, my sideline experience with the Revlon Run/Walk. I really did ease into my commitment to embrace breast cancer and the responsibility that comes with survivorhood.

One day, the senior producer of the *Today* show fourth hour, Amy Rosenblum, asked me, "Why don't we make a ring for you that says FORWARD?" She knew it was the word I'd kept writing in my journal. There were dozens of bracelets out: LIVE STRONG, SUPPORT OUR TROOPS, ORGAN DONATION, ANIMAL RIGHTS. Amy thought a ring would be special. I loved the idea. Dainty and powerful at the same time, my little pink rubber FORWARD ring was like my woobie. I wore it for two years straight, every day. It reminded me that I had made it through, and that I had to keep moving forward. We got a lot of requests from *Today* show viewers who wanted a ring for themselves or someone they loved. So, we began offering them for sale at the NBC Experience Store and online. Some of the profits go to Susan G. Komen for the Cure, so it makes a lot of sense. I don't wear my woobie everyday anymore, but I do pop it back on when I need a little comfort.

Slowly, after my story ran on the *Today* show, I began to make speeches about breast cancer. One of the first was a March 2008 Health Expo in Davenport, Iowa. It had been one year since my surgery. After that, Sheryl Crow's manager asked me to speak at an event for *Women & Cancer* magazine. I was later featured in the Summer 2008 issue.

Several months later, I was fly-fishing in rural New York with breast cancer survivors. The next month, I appeared at a health fair in Boston, followed by a speech at the New Orleans Press Club. You get the idea. Now, I give an average of about twelve speeches throughout the year, mostly on weekends. I travel anywhere from the Cayman Islands to the Quad Cities to commencements. I talk for about fifteen minutes and then chat with people afterward for as long as the group wants. I love to share that time with the women and men who attend. I try to give it my all when I'm able to participate in an event, because unfortunately, I do have to say no to some requests.

In June of 2009, I was asked to be the honorary chair of the Komen St. Louis Race for the Cure. I did *not* expect the turnout or the hoopla that this city generates. Wow! All of downtown was bathed in pink, including the water in the stone fountains. My job was to start the 5K race, and when they hoisted me up in a cherry

Pink power

picker, the view took my breath away. An ocean of people stretched out before me, survivors in pink T-shirts, the remaining participants in white. Over a loudspeaker, they called out for the one-year survivors, then the five-year, then the ten-, even the twenty-. By the time they got to the thirty-year survivors, I just wanted to get down on my knees and sob. It was emotional and beautiful and overwhelming. I tried from my swaying white bucket to make eye contact with individual faces; to call out names I could read on T-shirts. Starting that race was an honor and a thrill. I watched hundreds of people stream by for a while, then I got down from my bucket and joined in the race.

Now you know how I lost a breast. Now I know what I've gained—some very important lessons. One is: Life has margins and should be valued, not wasted. Banging around in my head is, *Not one more minute. I will not waste one more minute.* Another is: Hold on tightly to the things you love. And get rid of the things you don't.

I've also walked away with four words. Four *wonderful* words. If you survive breast cancer or any other illness or any tragedy, you get the gift of these words: *You can't scare me.*

How perfect. How powerful.

And you know what? Those four little words are what landed me the fourth hour of the *Today* show.

P.S.

Among the many songs that lifted my spirits during this tough year was "Anyway" cowritten and performed by Martina McBride. On the hardest of days, this song inspired me to believe—anyway. You may want to track it down for your next tough day.

PART FOUR

Life Without
Cue Cards

16

YOU CAN'T SCARE ME

There are employees who wait to be noticed. Maybe you work with someone who does. Maybe you wait yourself. I used to. I figured if I did my job well at *Dateline*, my bosses would see and I would be rewarded. I never asked for a promotion. Maybe I was afraid to ask. Afraid to be rejected. But things changed. After my cancer surgery, the New Me was fearless. I had survived cancer and I was armed with my four wonderful words: *You can't scare me.* Suddenly, talking to my bosses about a possible promotion seemed so small, so nothing. I wanted to be considered for the new fourth hour of the *Today* show. And I was going to say it out loud.

I made an appointment with the CEO of NBC Universal, Jeff Zucker. I told him about the New Me—the four words, the fearless thing. I told him I wanted to host the new hour of the *Today* show. I told him why I would be good, what I brought to the table. I just needed a shot. Jeff listened and said he would think about it. Next, I headed down to the third floor of 30 Rock and met with Steve Capus, president of the News Division, and gave the same speech again. I was not afraid, not nervous—none of it. *I did it!* I asked for it.

In the meantime, I continued work at *Dateline* and also filled in a bit on the nine o'clock hour and at the news desk of *Today*. At that time, the *Today* show was doing well but being tweaked by a 5-foot triple shot of espresso named Amy Rosenblum. Her energy is endless and so are her ideas. (Just like her idea for my FORWARD ring!) When Amy talks, you just bump along on the white caps churning atop her stream of consciousness. Amy is the woman people hire when they want to change a room. She tells it like it is and what it's going to be like from now on. NBC hired her to shake up the comfortably number one *Today* show and make it even better. As you might imagine, she's not always the most popular gal in the room. That's the down side of being exceptionally good at reconstruction.

One morning, I was filling in on the nine o'clock hour of *Today*, preparing to interview a guest about a serious topic I've since forgotten. In the two-minute break, I was saying hello to the guest and looking over my notes.

Right then, Amy walked up and said, "They think you're boring."

Stunned, I said, "What?"

"They think you're boring. Be the girl you are in my office."

Standby!

And we were live.

And there I went, boring me, interviewing some guest about who knows what, because I was wondering how not to be boring during a serious interview. What the hell just happened?! I got Amy-ed. That's what happened. And enlightened. Boy, I would have never guessed that was the "knock" on me. I always felt like I was being safe, following the rules, getting it right. Who wouldn't want that in a journalist? As I thought about it, NBC never told me anything was great or anything was bad. Just solid. No traction. In my defense, I guess I was trying to navigate between what I know now as serious *Dateline* Hoda and fun *Today* show Hoda. The compromise, though, was safe Hoda. (And apparently, boring Hoda.) In her office, Amy saw someone who could handle the new fourth hour. She wanted me to see it, and she wanted others to see it, too.

Serendipitously, the New Me talk I had with my bosses about the fourth hour was getting reenforced by Amy's behind-the-scenes push for me for the job. She had been promoted to oversee the new fourth hour. Amy says this is how a meeting about the fourth hour played out with the NBC bosses:

"I think Hoda would be good for the fourth hour," said Amy.

Hmm. The bosses said they weren't sure.

"Strap on your vaginas, boys, and listen to me," said the pistol.

Thankfully, Jim Bell, the new executive producer of the *Today* show, backed me, too. A few weeks later, I got a call from Steve Capus's assistant saying Steve wanted me to come to his office. I raced over.

He said, "I have a question for you, Hoda. Do you want to host the fourth hour of the *Today* show?"

Yes! Yes! Yes!

I called Amy to let her know the news. Her response was hilarious—a mix of happiness, sarcasm, and pride: "You were wandering the halls of NBC for *nine years* before I came along." Amy *still* says that now when she sees me, the former hapless nomad of NBC.

17

THE FOURTH HOUR

When the fourth hour of the *Today* show hit the airwaves, the couch cushions were covered by news gals: Ann Curry, Natalie Morales, and me. We were basically all the same girl in terms of our willingness to give, or in this case, *not* give personal opinions about topics. We're just not wired like that (and for good reason), when it comes to the impartial news business. But this fourth hour was supposed to be about discussing topics in a loose and fun way. Yet for us, any hint of an opinion felt like we were not maintaining the "brand" of NBC and practicing solid journalism. Sometimes we added new folks to the couch, like *Today* show correspondent Tiki Barber or celebrity chef Giada De Laurentiis. But no one was drawing anyone out, and that was a recipe for dull on many days. This new adventure was quite a challenge, from what to say to what to wear.

One month into the show, Stacy London, fashion consultant and cohost of TLC's *What Not to Wear,* was brought in to help me. I'd never worked on a daily program where fashionable clothes were required. I knew I did not have enough clothes. Look, I've just never been a shopper. Clothes aren't my thing. I find a few things I love, and I wear the crap out of them. During my fashion intervention with Stacy (which aired on our fourth hour), we showcased how clothes-blind I am by using a revealing montage of my overexposed orange sweater (which I still love!):

Me on the Air: Whenever I got the call to fill in on the *Today* show, I'd think, *I know what I'm going to wear tomorrow. I'll wear my orange sweater.*

Video Archive: Kotb wears orange sweater as she sits on *Today* show couch with Al Roker and Natalie Morales. Roker says, "Hoda's got on her lucky sweater . . ."

Video Archive: Kotb with Matt Lauer in Ireland as they hold mugs of beer and toast as she wears the same "lucky sweater."

Cheers to my orange sweater!

Good lord. What can I say. That's just me.

So, Stacy took me shopping at Saks Fifth Avenue (just like squeaky-pants Lisa!) and offered advice on finding clothes that flattered my skin tone, body type, and age.

We got my clothes fixed, but the rest of the ensemble was still a work in progress. We did our best each morning to create a chattier atmosphere. High-energy Amy Rosenblum was our fourth-hour leader, and she was constantly out on the floor, flailing her arms and giving us direction. She created several brilliant franchises for our hour, like "The Joy Fit Club" (someone who'd lost 100 pounds or more) and the "Ambush Makeover" (someone from the crowd is pulled into the studio for an instant makeover).

One afternoon, Amy and I were eating lunch at Michael's, a popular Midtown restaurant. I happened to look across the room and see a beautiful woman who I thought was Kathie Lee Gifford. "Amy, is that Kathie Lee Gifford?" I knew her only from watching *Live with Regis and Kathie Lee* years earlier.

Amy looked over and confirmed, "Yes! That's her." Amy's wheels began spinning. "We should have her cohost the show!"

I thought it was a fun idea. So we walked over to Kathie Lee's table, where she was sitting with a friend and we introduced ourselves. "We miss you on TV, Kathie Lee! How would you like to cohost our show in November?"

Kathie Lee was very polite and told us she'd ask her assistant (and closest friend), Christine, to check her schedule. A few days later, Christine contacted NBC to confirm that Kathie Lee was available to cohost for a morning. We were very excited!

On November 14, 2007, Ann, Natalie, and I made room on the couch for Kathie Lee. None of us thought to strap on a seat belt. We should have, because instantly, you could feel the show lurch—in a good direction. As if someone had sprinkled in the perfect spice to make our mix more delicious. The fun began the minute we went live.

ME: How does it feel waking up so early again?

KLG: Oh, you know I came in from Connecticut and I was thinking, *How did I do this all those years?* But then you get here and people start primping you and telling you how great you look. That's how I did it—by people lying to me the entire time.

As the cameras rolled, so too did Kathie Lee—with everything from discussing the Drew Peterson case, to cougars who date younger men, to fielding questions from the audience.

WOMAN: I want to know what you do to stay in shape.

KLG: Well, thank you. I have gained about ten pounds since I left *Live with Regis and Kathie Lee*, and so I wear those Spanx things that are so great. But I do Pilates every day and try to walk two miles a day. And then I have a smart-mouthed son that I chase around. I actually broke my finger the other day, chasing him. So, you know, I think having children still at home gives me a reason to get up in the morning, too. Although I am creaky in the morning. I'm very gnarly. I'm becoming gnarly.

We were all in awe of her ability to let it fly. She brought exactly what our hour needed. She didn't have the shackles of news; she said what she thought (her favorite line is "I don't give a rip!"), and she's a twenty-year veteran of live talk television.

That morning, NBC correspondent Janet Shamlian joined us for a segment on creating a lovely holiday photo card. She got a double shot of Kathie Lee.

JANET:	Every year I think, *We didn't get it, it didn't work, no one was looking at the camera,* and then this year . . .
ME:	The big reveal . . . let's see . . .
JANET:	We got one! [*We show a shot of Janet's Christmas photo card.*]
ME:	Yay!
KLG:	Gorgeous.
JANET:	This year's holiday card.
ME:	Everybody's smiling!
KLG:	It's a little too much cleavage for Christmas, but maybe that's just me.
ME:	All right. [*Nervous laugh*]
KLG:	More of a Happy New Year card . . .

The crowd and crew exploded into laughter, but we news gals were a bit nervous. *Did she just say "cleavage" on our show?!* We were shocked. It seemed like we'd go to news jail just because we were in the same room with that word. Boy, were we wrong. After the show, a man who rarely crosses the street crossed the street. Phil Griffin, a big gun in the NBC News Division, walked over from his building to 30 Rock and into Studio 1A. He said, "I love *this* show."

I knew something big was happening. As Kathie Lee was leaving, I joked with her, "See you tomorrow." She laughed.

I thought surely she must have enjoyed tapping into her gift again.

18

KATHIE LEE

After Kathie Lee's visit, I continued working on *Dateline* stories and cohosting the fourth hour. Ann was extremely busy with a grueling schedule, hosting four hours of the *Today* show plus covering stories all over the world. Natalie was promoted to cohost of the nine o'clock hour and was also the national correspondent. I began to hear through back channels that NBC was talking with Kathie Lee about permanently cohosting the fourth hour alongside me. Among other concerns about reentering TV after an eight-year hiatus, she was adamant about getting to know me better before she signed on for the job. A lunch was set up where we could relax and talk.

Let's just say, somewhere over the Rainbow Room, the deal was basically sealed. NBC did not want any eyes on our meeting, so I was brought up a back way into the Rainbow Room. (It's closed now, but at the time it was a historic, upscale restaurant and nightclub on the sixty-fifth floor of the GE Building in Rockefeller Center overlooking

Midtown Manhattan.) Kathie Lee was also escorted up through a secret entrance. Seems excessive, but the Peacock knows best. Once we sat down and the food was served and the wine was poured, the clock took a lunch break, too. I don't know what happened, but time forgot to register, and suddenly our afternoon lunch turned into predinner preparations unfolding all around us. We were four hours into our meeting! Kathie Lee had a million interesting stories, I opened up about my breast cancer and divorce and she sang to me in the restaurant. She told me about the "Everyone Has a Story" idea she had for the show (a segment we now feature monthly), and I was completely sold. We laughed, we cried, we connected. I felt like she was real.

A few days later, Kathie Lee invited me to her house in Connecticut to meet Frank (whom she always refers to as Frank Gifford) and her kids. Again, it was important for her to gauge our compatibility and connection before she came on board. When I arrived for dinner, I was, of course, overwhelmed by the beauty of her home. But, at the risk of sounding corny, I was more blown away by whom I met there. I loved Frank instantly. He was kind, funny, gracious, fit, and as I would learn over the months, bred with those old school manners you don't find much anymore. I'll never forget watching him at a work lunch we all attended several years ago and thinking, *This is a real man.*

The event was for the Salvation Army and Kathie Lee was the MC. We NBC folks had our own table, and our senior producer, Tammy Filler, was arriving late. As she walked in and was maneuvering through the crowd toward the table, Frank got up from his seat, scooted around, and pulled out Tammy's chair. He tucked her in and walked back to his seat. The telling part was that Kathie Lee didn't look at him, like, "Oh, Frank, thank you!" Rather, it was just known that this is what he does—this is who he is all the time. Frank 101.

Before dinner at their house that night, Frank and I chatted about his days sportscasting on *Monday Night Football*. After a few minutes, he pointed at Kathie Lee and cooed, "She's a legend, this one. She is the most loyal person I've ever met and the most trustworthy. I don't know you, but if you trust her and she trusts you, this will work." That was the biggest takeaway for me that night. Frank basically said that when Kathie Lee is all in, she's *really* in. And I can see that. She's surrounded by long-term relationships. All the people Kathie Lee loves have been in her life for more than twenty years. Her driver, her assistant, her closest friends. Loyalty and commitment are huge to her. I now understood our lunch at the Rainbow Room and dinner at her home.

On a side note: I've since seen many examples of Kathie Lee's loyalty to friends and family. One evening, we were in the city together

KLG and me in Ocean Reef, Florida, 2009

listening to cabaret. A random man approached us and began talking to her. Somehow, in passing, the man said how much he did *not* like watching Bill O'Reilly on television. Kathie Lee told him that, in fact, Bill was a friend of hers. Well, the man just kept on, saying very negative things about Bill. I continued to watch as Kathie Lee politely but firmly reiterated her point to the man. She touched his arm, looked him in the eye and said again that Bill O'Reilly was a friend of hers. She could have simply listened to his rant and let it go. But instead, she worked to kindly stand him down and stand up for her friend. Loyalty.

On top of all that good stuff during the Gifford dinner, I liked Kathie Lee's kids. They're smart, fun, and polite. If Kathie Lee had her way, Cody's first word would've been "please" and Cassidy's "thank you." She and Frank were determined to raise their kids well and it shows. On the drive home that night, I felt like she and I could work. Nothing felt forced. Now, in all honesty, I did have plenty of concern about the potential for—how shall I say—a credibility suck. The fourth hour with Kathie Lee would demand a daily dose of fun and frivolity. I'd worked very hard over the years developing a solid set of credentials in the news business, and was unclear on how I'd manage the mix of interviewing dirty politicians *and* running an obstacle course in an inflatable sumo wrestler costume. I've garnered a few awards that I'm proud of: an Alfred I. duPont, a Peabody, and an Edward R. Murrow Award. So, I had to wonder—do they strip you of those if you're later spotted on the air playing "How Much Can You Stuff in Your Spanx?"

I called my agent, Carole Cooper, and asked her opinion about taking this direction and how it could impact twenty years of hard work—if it didn't work. She wisely pointed out that it's a new world now, one where viewers accept crossover. She gave the examples of Anderson Cooper starting out as host of *The Mole* and moving on to anchor the news at CNN. She also cited Meredith coanchoring the *Today* show and also hosting *Who Wants to Be a Millionaire.* I felt Carole was right, but my excitement about this new opportunity was definitely mixed with apprehension.

Kathie Lee and I were not allowed to talk to each other until all the paperwork was complete. When the secret deal was finally done, she called me on my cell phone and said, "Okay, when we get out of this NBC Witness Protection Program, I'm going to be your cohost." It was crazy! Who'd have thought I'd be cohosting a morning talk show with Kathie Lee Gifford? I'm sure she was thinking the same thing about me, having already cohosted an Emmy-nominated talk show for fifteen years. But, just five months after she filled in on the fourth hour, Kathie Lee was now the official cohost.

Our first show together aired live in April of 2008 outside of 30 Rock on the Plaza. I can take credit for the idea of doing our show outside, because it turned out to be a bad one. The idea was: we'll know if things are "working" by using the crowd as a barometer of sorts—a laugh-o-meter. Embracing the energy of onlookers seemed like a smart decision. What we didn't anticipate was—*the noise!* The noise level on the Plaza was intense—and we loved it—but we could barely hear each other, let alone the guests. Also, you just don't consider how difficult it is to do a serious interview with a giant hamburger head, foam fingers, and a tour group from Latvia behind you. Here was another snag: not only could we not hear each other, the crowd couldn't hear us. We were not allowed to broadcast our exterior audio at a loud level because apparently, people are *working* in all the buildings that surround the Plaza. The nerve! The whole beautiful concept of holding our show outside was a bust. It's like when you have the image of a perfect picnic in your head—and then it sucks. Blowing napkins, ants, and wet grass.

We stuck it out for a month, and then the most gorgeous straw that ever broke the camel's back showed up on our set. Producers booked Mexican actor Eduardo Verástegui, star of the fabulous independent film *Bella*. Okay, this man is ridiculously bellissimo. The sight of him takes your breath away. You simply want to spread him on a cracker. And so, that morning, when the ManGod walked outside onto our set, the crowd exploded. (That's all you can do when you see Eduardo.) Instantly, the decibel level on the Plaza skyrocketed to the heavens—like some sort of audio orgasm. *Kaboom!*

The guys in charge of the building went ballistic. "Shut it down! You are shutting this show *down!*" Men were actually dragging away our chairs and herding us off the set. But, y'know what? If you're gonna go out, Eduardo is a pretty sweet swan song.

Have I mentioned how magnificent he is?

May 6 was our last day outside. Our poor producers had to beg the building guys for one last special favor: to let us set up a $3,000 gardening segment we had scheduled for outdoors and simply could not fit indoors. They agreed, but only if we would *shh* the crowd during the broadcast. And we did.

ME:	We are going outside, and we are going to make some nice outdoor rooms for you.
KLG:	But no noise.
ME:	No noise. We'll be *shh, shh, shh, shh, shh.*

Looking back, I learned one of my most valuable lessons during our stint outside on the Plaza. And Kathie Lee was the one who taught it to me. Working in news for so long, I was very comfortable with scripts and the little device we wear in our ears called an IFB. The IFB allows you to hear directions from folks in the control room.

"We don't have the tape, so just know that you guys will be on camera for the rest of the segment" is something you might hear.

Or, "Eduardo is back to ask you to marry him, Hoda."

Okay, not that, but you get the idea.

The IFB and scripts for me are just part of how I do my job. But when the set was outside, scripts became small index cards because it was so windy. And Kathie Lee didn't wear an IFB because it just wasn't a tool she used during her years in TV. One morning, our show was just not popping. My cards were blowing around, the energy wasn't there, and I was frustrated. Finally, Kathie Lee said to me live on the air (of course): "Would you just get rid of those darn cards? Just *toss* them. Toss them!"

I almost tossed my cookies instead. I refused at first, white-knuckling my paper security blankets. But finally, I did it. I tossed those cards up into the air (*on* the air) and thought I would die. But, actually, the show went much more smoothly and I liked the concept. I eventually took out my IFB, too. (The control room was not that happy about me cutting the umbilical cord, but we managed.) Kathie Lee has single-handedly stripped me of my news corset and taught me how to just let it all hang out. I will tell you this—she makes it look a lot easier than it is. We still have small cards that producers print for us with topic notes, but she really has enlightened me on being less guarded and more open to showing the real me and accepting the consequence that not everybody's going to like it. Oddly enough, the "toss your cards" lesson has actually crossed over into my other world and improved my *Dateline* interviews. I used to be married to the question list that I'd bring with me after researching a story. I knew right where I wanted the interview to go. "So, therefore, interviewee, we're going down this path." The person I was interviewing could take me on a turn, but I would try to veer us back onto my course. But now (toss your cards here) I'm more present and I pay attention. I don't refer to my question sheet as often. I even tuck it under my leg now when I do *Dateline* interviews. I listen better and stop thinking ahead.

I'm often asked, "What's Kathie Lee *really* like?"

It's funny, at the beginning I really didn't know. We hit the air-waves without even one rehearsal. Would she be a diva? Is she a hard-worker? Would she be nice to people behind the scenes?

Here's what I now know. Kathie Lee is not a diva. She's always on time and she comes to play. She asks everyone about their family and friends and keeps up with all the happenings. She sings to me every morning when she strolls into the makeup room to the tune of "Oklahoma!" (Where, of course, you now know I was born.)

"Hoooooooooooooooooda woman, where the wind comes sweepin' down the plain . . ."

Kathie Lee is funny, generous, opinionated, and passionate. Her brain is always in overdrive. If you get in the back seat of her car, there's invariably a notepad stuck in the back pocket of the passenger seat, along with pens and five pairs of glasses. She's always writing something. When I ask her what she has planned for the weekend, the answer is never what most of us would say. It's always: "Well, I'm gonna finish that song I've been working on, and, oh my gosh . . . I've got this great idea for a children's book . . . and I'm reading this thing that is *so* fascinating . . ." Kathie Lee has an active, curious, creative brain. There's no downtime for her and that's how she likes it. I remember when we wrapped up our show live from San Antonio, "Welcome to San Antonio, Ain't It Fun," and we were all pooped. We had flown into San Antonio late at night, woken up very early to tape some segments before the show, did the show, and then tried to fly out, only to have several flight delays. When we finally boarded, I looked over to see Kathie Lee starting a new book. On that flight, she read *The Eleventh Victim* by Nancy Grace. *Then* I caught her reading the back flap of the book because she had nothing else to do. I, on the other hand, could barely stay awake and was flipping through *Star* magazine.

"What's it like sitting next to her?" people often ask me, too. Well, for one thing, I sit next to Kathie Lee on her right side because the left chair (screen right) was always hers when she worked with Regis. It's like sleeping on the usual side of the bed for her. And for me, it's a little like sitting next to Regis. Kathie Lee has settled nicely into the role of Velvet Barb Thrower. And I'm the bull's-eye.

"So, were you really divorced on Valentine's Day?" she asked me during one of our very first days on the air.

That's what it's like sitting next to her.

But, here's the bottom line: Kathie Lee is very funny and she has a knack for targeting stuff that sticks. For instance, she nicknamed me "Hoda Woman." She calls me her "Egyptian Goddess." She thinks I have pretty feet. So, you can imagine my surprise when all that crazy stuff connects with viewers.

"Hey, Hoda Woman!" a truck driver will shout at me along Broadway. "Nice feet!"

I smile and just laugh at the power of KLG.

"Wow, I didn't realize you were from Egypt," someone else will say on the street.

Can Kathie Lee be a pain in my ass? Yes. Some days I want to take her to the mat and stick gum in her hair. But, love her or hate her, Kathie Lee knows how to do live talk television. And don't worry about me, I can take whatever she dishes. Would you really want to

At home with Kathie Lee

watch a show where we held a meeting of the Mutual Admiration Society every day? Dull. A colleague once told me, in a television duo there can't be two drivers because there'll be a head-on crash. There has to be an actor and a reactor. (Guess which one I am?) As the actor cog, Kathie Lee catches some flack for her outspoken wit. The actor part of the team usually pays that price. I just get to react and deflect, so I don't take the same heat. And for me, it's all about intent. I know Kathie Lee has a golden heart and she has my back. So, cracks she makes about me are simply done in good fun. Her intentions are good. Like when your brother ribs you. Plus, I really don't have many Achilles' heels for her words to penetrate.

"Oh, a study about dating," she'll say on the air. "Remember what that is, Hoda Woman?"

But I do date! So that doesn't bother me. It's a joke.

"Well, you could wear that, Hoda Woman," she'll point out. "You're a bigger girl."

My weight is not an issue for me, either. I'm 5 feet 9 and weigh around 150 pounds. Put me down for a size 8 or sometimes a 10.

Sneaky math never occurs to me. Weight is just not a hot button. In fact, during my life, it probably should have been on my radar screen a bit more. I look back at work photos and am shocked. Was I eating the people I was interviewing?! Good Lord, I was big. Back when I worked in Greenville, Mississippi, with good old Stan as my news director, he actually tried to ease into the topic with me. "Hey, Hoda," Stan began. "You may want to think about (picture Stan now beginning to swing his bent arms back and forth in a workout motion) getting on the treadmill . . ." I laughed! I thought Stan was joking around with me. That crazy Stan!

These days, I'm more aware of keeping a healthy weight and lifestyle, but again—viewers need not worry that Kathie Lee's jabs are anything but good fun (and good TV). Plus, I get to pop her during those *Saturday Night Live* skits!

Have you seen those? They crack me up. And what's even funnier is Kathie Lee's take on them.

"That is *nothing* like our show," she'll say.

Are you kidding me? They are spot-on, with a delectable dose of satire.

In January of 2009, on the Thursday the *Saturday Night Live* cast was rehearsing the very first skit about us, an NBC colleague came into our makeup room and said, "Hey, *SNL* is doing a spoof on the *Today* show," he laughed. "And it's sort of specifically about you two." Kathie Lee had been spoofed before during her *Live with Regis and Kathie Lee* days, but I wondered what the heck they would do about us. "Are we gonna think it's funny?" I asked. I didn't care how I was portrayed, but I was terrified that cast member Kenan Thompson, a burly black guy, would be in drag—playing me. "Oh, yeah," he said. "You'll think it's funny."

That Saturday night, I watched the bit hit the air. What a weird

Cheers to *SNL*!

6 minutes and 23 seconds. I grew up watching *SNL*—now this?! The skit was hilarious. Kristin Wiig played Kathie Lee brilliantly (sorry, Kath), and Michaela Watkins was a very good me. The jokes, of course, targeted my name, with Kathie Lee calling me "Ho" and "Yoda." She popped her Spanx under her dress and talked about Frank on a Hoveround. I mostly just sat there as Kathie Lee elbowed me and said I had no man in my life. Nothing like our show? *Right.*

Neil Patrick Harris then appeared in our segment as a fitness guru and brought down the house. He was dressed in a headband and tights under short shorts. We followed along in our dresses and heels as he barked out aerobics moves. "Now, box step, and box step . . . now crunk it, and crunk it . . . now grapevine, and grapevine, now double time, double time . . ." Then, at 5 minutes and 55 seconds— the money shot. Neil Patrick Harris began instructing us to "Punch it out . . . now punch it out . . . punch it out . . ." Kathie Lee shuffled over next to me, and that's when I let loose.

Punch line!

Bam!

I socked it to her, right in the jaw! She flew across the room.

Watching at home, I knew I'd have to milk that right hook for all it was worth. The next morning, during the show, I had producers replay and replay and replay the video.

"Hey, guys . . . let's see that again." I smiled.

Bam!

SNL spoofed us several more times. I saw Kristin Wiig in the hall one day, and she said, "Did you guys think it was funny or are you mad at us?" I told her we loved it! She is so nice and so damn funny. I know Kathie Lee would have told her the same thing. KLG can hardly be thin-skinned, considering how she "brings it." And she brings it with great skill. Honestly, one of the most unique strengths she offers our hour is her magic with guests. I never anticipated how much of a shortcut her entertainment background would bring to the interview process.

Here's how it works: She's one of them. Kathie Lee is viewed by our guests as a woman in *their* business, not a newswoman who wants to ask some tough questions. Her background as a singer, actress, musical theater composer, author, and entertainer creates an instant common ground. Plus, she has a history with so many of the people we invite on our show that she rarely, like most of us, has to start from ground zero. If Beyoncé is our guest, Kathie Lee already knows her because she interviewed her when she was just starting out with Destiny's Child. The dynamic is amazing. We don't have to spend time with the typical warm-up questions, because there's no need to break the ice.

"So, how much plastic surgery *have* you had?" she'll ask. That's her ice-breaker. And the guests love it.

I remember watching Judi Dench's face, searching for how this classy, superstar actress would react to Kathie Lee's particular brand of humor. We were interviewing Judi for her role in the movie *Nine,* and she was telling us about a certain part of the movie that she couldn't show us due to movie rights.

"It must be because you were naked, right?" said Kathie Lee.

I watched—and waited—and regal Judi Dench threw her head back and burst out laughing. Only Kathie Lee can pull that off.

"So, how many wives have you *really* had?" she asked one of our guests.

And then—the magic.

"C'mon, Kath. You know I've had *five,*" laughed the guest. "You were at *two* of the weddings."

I think part of the energy that makes it work is that these folks are used to getting their asses kissed. So, finally, when someone says something that's a bit irreverent, they find it refreshing. Plus, Kathie Lee has perfect pitch for whom she can play with.

"I like your dress . . . ," she said one morning to Cheryl Hines, an actress from the hit show *Curb Your Enthusiasm*.

". . . but it's not . . . really . . . age appropriate," Kathie Lee added.

Again, I waited—and I watched—and Cheryl burst out laughing.

Believe me—we're prepared for times when a guest or viewers may not embrace the humor of KLG. In the control room, producers have access to a "CYA" button that, when pressed, crawls the following across the bottom of the screen: "We would like to apologize for what she just said, what she is currently saying, and for what she is about to say."

The level of fun that Kathie Lee and I are allowed to have is scary and wonderful at the same time. Someone told me that at an annual NBC gathering of advertisers, NBC Universal president and CEO Jeff Zucker began talking about the faces of the *Today* show.

"So, as you know," Jeff began, "we've got Meredith, Matt, Al, and Ann covering the first few hours, then Natalie joins in at the nine o'clock hour, *and then we have those crazy bitches at ten!*"

That's right. And the crazy bitches would like to place all the blame on comedienne Chelsea Handler. Sometime after she was a guest on our hour, we began to drink more often on the air. The morning she appeared, our producers decided to make three vodka drinks for us in Chelsea's honor. She was pitching her new book, *Are You There, Vodka? It's Me, Chelsea*. We had so much fun that day that we decided to sample some libations on another show, too. Our guest was a wine expert and we took our glasses with us into the next unrelated segment. Then, all of a sudden, we were featuring Wines Under Seven Dollars off the top of the show. We knew when *Time* magazine called our hour "The Happy Hour" that a theme had developed. And that's really what we try to be (not in a boozy way)—an escape from all the bad news reported around the world. We're escape artists.

Happy Winesday

There's still a part of me that struggles with it. I'm a news gal who spends more of her job now talking about cleavage and sipping cocktails on air. My mom called me one day and said, "It's weird, my friends are saying you are drinking all the time." She tried to make her voice have a smile in it. "But I told them, 'She only has one.' Right?" I could tell she was worried and trying to get reassurance. "I told them it was just for the show . . . right?"

I had to laugh, because I don't drink a lot. Never have. But, I can see where our ten o'clock hydrating could send a different—burp—message.

"Mom, I only drink on the air."

That's reassuring, eh? Mom, just tell your friends your daughter only likes to get boozy in front of 2 million viewers. It's funny, I seem to take more heat from people for how much *I* eat on the show rather than for how much *we* drink.

"You *always eating!*" says my nail gal to me. "You *eat, eat, eat!*"

Yes. We eat, we drink—and we go to Broadway. We are *very* cultured. Or I should say, Kathie Lee is very cultured. I would venture to say that the only thing that rivals Kathie Lee's passion for Frank Gifford is her passion for the Great White Way. This woman's internal compass points her directly to the theater district. And she wants to take me and you right along with her. One of her requests for cohosting our hour was that she could shine more light on the passionate and insanely talented people who make up Broadway. She has already written two musicals: *Under the Bridge*, which was produced Off-Broadway, and *Saving Aimee*, which had its world-premiere production at the Signature Theatre in Shirlington, Virginia, in 2007. For countless years, she's been rewriting the musical as *The Seduction of Sister Aimee*, hoping one day soon she'll watch it being performed on a Broadway stage. Kathie Lee herself is no stranger to the stage. She performed as the orphan-hating Miss Hannigan in the 2006 production of *Annie* at Madison Square Garden.

Before I met Kathie Lee, my exposure to Broadway was very typical—*Cats, Phantom of the Opera, The Lion King*. Now, I go just about every week with Kathie Lee and her dear friend Sunny Luciani. We have lunch before, then head to the show. I have to say—there are times I'm lost. "Is he *really* dead now?" I'll whisper to Sunny. "Or is this a *pretend* ghost?" In the meantime, Kathie Lee is on top of it all and in her element. Her enthusiasm is contagious. She has broadened my Broadway chops and our viewers', too. You just don't realize the quality of the live performances until you sit in those seats. The musicals are my favorite, but it's all impressive. Live, no second chances, always distractions for the performers. One afternoon, we were seated in front of two older folks with misbehaving hearing aids. All we heard was, "Beeeeeeeepppppp, booooooooopppppp, beeeeeeeeepppppp!"

I could barely keep it together and was amazed that actor James Spader didn't snap and call them out. We actually moved our seats during intermission, only to have the couple move, too. *Right behind us!*

"Beeeeeeeeppppppp, boooooooooppppppp, beeeeeeeeeppppppp!"

Broadway doesn't tolerate interruptions, but I guess hearing aids are rightfully off-limits. But, FYI—don't ever unwrap candy during a show. People look at you like you're skinning a cat.

When Kathie Lee and I are out at a show or anywhere together, women often ask us about our wardrobe. Does someone pick out your clothes? Do you two actually coordinate your outfits? Where do I get my bracelets and earrings? (Jennifer Miller Jewelry, by the way). The decision was made early on that I would wear dresses. One thing to put on, add some shoes, pop on jewelry. Zip and go. Kathie Lee is such a lady that dresses are a perfect fit for her. So, we both keep all of our outfits at work—dresses, shoes, and accessories. (My mom is responsible for many of the dresses I wear on air. She has a perfect size record with me. A dress will arrive in a box in my apartment lobby, and I just take it right in the box to work. I know it will fit and look good. Thanks, Mom!) The challenge for me is remembering what the hell I wore and when I wore it. You know when someone says they like your earrings and you have to touch them to remember what pair you have on? That's how I am with everything I wear. I'm oblivious. But I'll tell you who remembers *everything* I wear: the viewers! On our Facebook page for the show, viewers have written: "Someone *please* buy Hoda a new pair of earrings! She's worn these for about two months straight!!!"

Or: "*Stop* wearing that red dress with the red V!"

And: "*Please, please, please* retire that red dress!"

But I *love* that dress! (Orange sweater syndrome.) I actually called viewers out on that one, saying on air the next day, "What are you talking about? I don't wear that red dress all the time . . ."

Big mistake, Hoda.

That comment spurred our producers to put together a montage of all the days I wore that damn red dress with the V. They got me. There was nothing I could do but retire that beauty to my closet at home. Now, whenever I start to wear a dress a little too often, our crew guys say, "Oh, Lord, this is gonna be like that red one."

Sadly, a "system" had to be developed for me. Donna Richards, our superefficient wardrobe gal, created a sort of *Dressing for Dummies* calendar for me. She logs what I wear each day on the calendar, and my job is to check it each morning before I get dressed so I don't repeat too often. I usually pick out my "approved" dress and then Kathie Lee chooses a dress that coordinates. I've enjoyed the dress-up process more than I ever thought I would. It certainly helps that I have people guiding me every zip, clasp, and step of the way. We have excellent help with our hair and makeup, too.

The *Today* show makeup room is like the kitchen in most people's homes. It's where everyone congregates. While Meredith gets worked on in her dressing room by people she's been with for years, the rest of us are fluffed and buffed by the brilliant Mary Kahler (makeup) and Laura Castorino (hair) in the makeup room. The number of heads these gals work on each day is amazing. The talent rolls through according to their hour of the show. Ann is usually first, followed by Natalie, and then regular contributors like Dr. Nancy Snyderman or celebrity chef Giada De Laurentiis. Kathie Lee and I are last to plop into the chairs.

My morning unfolds with a trip to the gym by 5 o'clock in the morning. I shower, then head to 30 Rock by 6:30. I go straight to the makeup room because it's the hot spot for what's making news and what's punching buttons.

"How are the people?" I'll ask each morning when I wander in.

The reply is always, "The people are good!"

During that hour, I listen to the banter and leaf through my pile of stuff—newspapers and information about my segments for the day's show. This is the faux meeting *before* the official meeting at 7:30. I'm listening for potential chat topics and determining what we all feel is the buzziest stuff. It's fun because everyone brings a different perspective to the same topic—just like the viewers who'll be watching. When it's my turn to pop into the chair, Laura spends about forty or forty-five minutes taming my most-often wet hair, followed by makeup for about the same amount of time. Kathie Lee is getting worked on next to me, and senior producer Tammy Filler, along with several of our hour's producers, have joined us in the makeup room as well. They suggest topics for us to use as springboards in the morning's chat segment.

"Okay, number one—John Edwards went to Haiti; number two—Tiger Woods was spotted; three—a study says women are waiting longer to get married," they throw out to us.

We spend time deciding if and how we can use each topic as a launching pad to additional topics, and whether we can move smoothly to the next one. We focus on developing happy, upbeat chat instead of the heavy stuff viewers have already watched for a few hours. If it's a huge news story, like the earthquake in Haiti, certainly we'll talk about it, but we'll steer the conversation toward positive stories of survivors or how to offer donations. The goal is to have fun and fill about ten to twelve minutes off the top of the show. When the producers leave the makeup room, I take my much-improved face and hair to my dressing room so I can read up on my show segments in private. You may be thinking, *Wow, there's actually show prep for your circus of an hour?*

Yes, there really is. If an author or actor or director comes on our show, we read as much of the book or see as much of the movie as time allows. The producers are great about getting us material days earlier, if possible. For example, when *Avatar* director James Cameron joined us, producers set up a special screening for us the day before so we'd be able to share our thoughts about the movie with him. I love that we also have the leeway to break away from the topic at hand and ask the guest for input on something we've discussed earlier in our chat segment.

"So, what side do you fall on? Jay or Conan?"

It's fun for us and our viewers to steer the guests off their paths for a minute, and then go right back to the project they're actually there to plug. Most days, the show flies by. We're done by 11 o'clock, and often I'm off and running to something else. I may go to a luncheon in the city where a colleague is either speaking or being honored. Sometimes I stay in the building to track audio scripts for a *Dateline* story I'm covering. Because I work two jobs now, coanchoring the fourth hour and as a correspondent for *Dateline,* I can't travel as often for interviews. Thankfully, *Dateline* frequently flies in the interviewees to New York. It makes sense in a lot of ways. Ideally, we interview people in their homes because you assume that's where they'd feel most comfortable. However, our crews are so good at what they do, they bring a truckload of gear to people's homes. They may have to rearrange and even relocate furniture onto the lawn to make room for all the lights, cameras, and audio equipment needed to create our consistently quality product. The result, though, is not-so-familiar surroundings anymore. What we do for me is fly in the interviewee, create a perfect setting in a New York hotel room, and conduct the interview from there. I try to schedule the sessions for noon, so I still have gas left in my tank. I get up at 4 A.M., so I don't want to run out of steam. It's been interesting having to switch gears now, with the two very different jobs. One minute I'm tooling around in a motorized cupcake, the next I'm firing questions at a convicted murderer.

Right around Halloween of 2009, the *Today* show decided to feature all of us as characters from the classic movie *Star Wars*. Matt was Luke Skywalker, Meredith was Princess Leia, Ann was Darth Vader, Al was Han Solo, Natalie was Queen Amidala, and Kathie Lee was C-3PO. With a name like Hoda, guess who I was? Yep. Yoda. My Jedi Master costume was nuts! Several days earlier, I had to sit with some sort of gunk on my face to create a custom-made rubber mask. My ears were—significant. Unfortunately, as timing would have it, in a galaxy far, far away, I had a *Dateline* interview after the show. I knew I wouldn't have much time to transform from Yoda to Hoda. When I arrived at the interview in a New York hotel room, I hoped I'd stripped off all remnants of Halloween. And I really hoped my *Dateline* interview hadn't flipped on the tube.

"Hey, I saw you this morning as Yoda!" I heard when I walked in the room.

Busted. My interview was a woman I'd profiled before for *Dateline* when she was convicted of murdering her husband. She was now out of prison on an overturned sentence, so we were doing a follow-up story. I laughed off the Yoda reference, grabbed my mental stick shift and switched gears. I do like the mix of hard news and fun news. It's interesting. I get to flex different muscles for work. Hard news I know and love—I'm a journalist first. But this new opportunity is great, too.

My work week is busy, but whose isn't? Two or three times a week I leave my heels on and head off to evening events. They're always for work, either giving a speech or MCing a gathering. I always request

From Hoda to Yoda

What, Ann? I can't hear you . . .

to be finished by 8:30 P.M. because that really means 9, and then I'm home by 9:30. My alarm clock buzzes at 4 A.M., so I try not to burn myself out as best I can. Once during the work week, I have a date or dinner with friends. By Friday, I'm tired and may not do a thing in the evening. Saturday and Sunday I always get in runs and usually have brunch with friends. I often go on another date one of the weekend evenings. Sometimes I travel to D.C. to see family, and then there's just the general stuff of life to tackle. I like the pace of my world. It's busy, but for me, the less I do the lazier I get. There's always room for improvement and a balance check, but overall, I'm doing just fine.

The studios for the *Today* show sit on three different floors. The top studio is for cooking segments and where Kathie Lee and I open our hour of the show. The middle floor is where most of what you watch on each hour happens. And the bottom floor is where the guests sit in the Green Room, awaiting their segments. You just don't know who or what you're going to run into on any of the floors.

Is that the woman who lost 100 pounds, or a model for the His & Hers Pajamas segment? I'll wonder.

Folks wandering about on the various floors are hard to identify. The Green Room is easier because people will introduce themselves.

"Hi, there. I'm the girl who can't stop sneezing."

Okay, wonderful! Thank you. Bless you.

The cast of characters for four hours of television is quite diverse, as you can imagine. I might see Morgan Freeman and Clint Eastwood standing next to the woman who's going to talk about the latest face creams. Oh, and there's Elton John. And while I'm introducing myself to the cervical cancer survivor, we might hear this boom over the loudspeakers: "Has anyone seen the flask that looks like a cell phone?"

I still think about the guest who had cervical cancer. She was jittery and told me several times that she was *very* nervous. Finally, I smiled at her and said, "Um . . . you beat cancer. Just a reminder." I paused. "You're going to talk to us for four minutes . . . you beat cancer." She laughed. And then she did a great job with her segment.

One thing I don't necessarily love seeing in the halls or on set are the creatures. If you've ever watched our hour, you know that I'm not great with furry things. Or things with scales—or shells—or beaks. On the days we have wild animals on set, I make sure Kathie Lee is *always* between me and the creatures.

"No, Hoda," she'll say. "That's *your* side."

19

THE BIG TOP

Filling four hours of quality morning television is a challenge. *Today* show producers have to come up with something interesting to talk about and someone interesting to talk to for hours on end, five days a week. And the process has to unfold, literally, like clockwork. While viewers are treated to a smooth, orderly experience on air, off air the studio halls are buzzing with activity. All the people and creatures that are "on deck" waiting for their turns are in a holding pattern behind the scenes. The best way to give you an idea of this is to share the kind of thing we typically hear crackling over the loudspeakers.

"Someone needs to get the cougar from 1A."

Or, "They need the big pants for the Joy Fit segment—STAT—to hang on the clothesline."

Then, the same voice will whisper, "Natalie, we need you in 1A, immediately."

It's a trip.

And I'll say, "Not today."

I don't enjoy the hair jumping. That's the issue. Animals look at me and see a comfortable place to nest.

"They go for the high places," the handler will say.

Yeah. I know it, and my lid knows it. I had a lemur in my hair so fast one morning I didn't even have time to react. I just stood there and let it knead around in the "habitat" for a while.

"Do they bite?!"

"Only if you provoke them," they always say.

I'm not doing anything! My hair is provoking them without my consent!

Birds love me. Macaws, spoonbills, vultures—you name it and I've likely housed it for several agonizing seconds. By now, I can spot it in their eyes.

Oh, God, here it comes! Flap, flap, flap—and perch.

I have learned a few tricks to at least outsmart the handlers.

"Put your hand out again," they'll say. "So he can eat more grapes."

"Ohhhh . . . (drop the grapes) . . . too bad—looks like I'm out of grapes."

I guess I'm just better with humans. They tend to move more slowly and almost never bite.

Incoming!!

20

GUESTS HOSTS
AND GUESTS

When someone's a guest in your home, you want them to enjoy them-selves. To laugh and eat and leave happy. We feel the same way about guests on our fourth hour. Except we don't own the home, we don't do the cooking or cleanup, and there are 2 million people looking through the windows. But we do our best to create a fun atmosphere for our guests. One thing I've learned about that process is that if I'm having fun, my guests are more apt to have fun. Sounds simple, but there *is* an art to Fun Management. I got a glimpse of how it works when I sat behind award-winning news correspondent and anchor Connie Chung back in August of 2004.

We were attending the largest gathering of journalists in the world, called UNITY: Journalists of Color, held in Washington, D.C. Every four years, the conference brings together thousands of journalists from all nationalities with the goal of improving diversity in the news. More than 8,000 people attended the year we were at the Washington Convention Center. I was asked to co-MC a meeting of the Asian American Journalists Association (What is you?) and was delighted to participate. The room was jam-packed with journalists, and we cohosts got up to introduce Connie, who was to make a speech.

"Ladies and gentlemen, Connie Chung."

Connie walked up to the podium and proceeded to tell the audience, "I have a little song for you guys." That year, both Senator John Kerry and then-President George W. Bush addressed the attendees. Connie felt inspired. She began to sing (to the tune of the song "Love and Marriage"), "Bush and Kerry, Bush and Kerry" . . . I can't recall the rest of the words, but I can remember how weird it felt. I had the perfect vantage point to see the audience, as I sat behind Connie and overlooked the crowd. I love to watch people give speeches. I love the ebb and flow and learning how good speakers grab and hold their listeners. But I have to tell you, I was a bit nervous for Connie. "Bush and Kerry, Bush and Kerry" . . . she sang with gusto. The faces in the crowd were blank. Arms were folded, some eyes were rolling.

Oh, my God! I worried. *Connie Chung is bombing!*

I wondered what the hell I would do if I was getting the same response to a fake song I was singing a cappella—and not that well. (Sorry, Connie.) I'm pretty sure I would have chalked up the loss and moved on. But Connie just kept belting it out. She didn't dial it back, she didn't retreat. In fact, she started singing louder. And then swinging her arms, inviting everyone to buy in. She sang, and smiled and sold it. And you know what? The crowd did buy in. By the end of that song, the place was howling. People were up on their feet and clapping wildly. Go figure.

I learned something that evening. There are times when you just have to show people that you're all in. Sometimes, if you're that far in, the best move is to go even farther and take everybody with you. That's Fun Management. After the speech, I told Connie how amazed I was by her approach and her calm. She shrugged it off. For her, it was just another day. She's a veteran who knows what she's doing and how to wrangle fun. She's a wise one.

Some of the guests we invite into our "home" are famous or familiar faces we ask to fill in for either me or Kathie Lee. When one of us takes time off or has to be away from the show, the roll call begins for a guest host. Because we are rarely gone, the fill-in experience is a bit odd for both of us—like being on a blind date. Clearly, it's even odder for the guest hosts. They are plucked out of their element and thrown into our world for an hour. I remember country music star Billy Ray Cyrus asking me in a southern drawl, "Do you want me to read the words over they-er"—pointing to the teleprompter—or "jist talk?" What a good guy. I told Billy Ray to just talk, and he did great.

We make a point to ease the guest hosts' nerves by chatting about their current projects and interests. One week, we invited a house-wife each day from the television series, *Real Housewives of (fill in the city)*. Bethenny Frankel, from *Real Housewives of New York*, was a very funny guest host and melded easily with the show. I asked her on air to tell us about some of the things she liked to do in New York City.

"I like to go to the Four Seasons and get this cotton candy treat," she described. "It's beautiful and fun."

I replied, "Wow, cotton candy at the Four Seasons—how much does that cost?"

She looked at me like I was nuts and without skipping a beat shot back, "You're on a date. It's free." Everything out of her mouth is hilarious. Like that.

We try to choose guest hosts who are current—people viewers recognize from a hot program or project. One of my favorite cohosts is Piers Morgan, known here in the United States as a judge on the TV program *America's Got Talent*. We like flirting with each other. He's British and witty and highly opinionated. Piers is also comfortable on set because he's familiar with the workings of television.

"Hoda, I'm engaged, but the door's still open," he'll say with his sexy accent and sly smile.

We had his fiancée on as a guest, and she's gorgeous and smart. So we get that Piers is harmless. The fun part is just having some testosterone around once in a while. The fourth hour is pretty heavily estrogen-laden. Piers always brings me on-air gifts, too, and tries to outgift his "rival" cohost, TV financial and advertising analyst Donny Deutsch. When Donny brought me a pair of Christian Louboutin designer shoes, Piers felt threatened—down in *his* pair. So, he called his friend, multibillionaire and Virgin founder Richard Branson. On the air, Piers handed me the phone.

"Hoda, we're offering you a trip to a private island," Branson said in his lovely accent.

I was thinking, *Oh, Lord—is that under $100? We can't accept big gifts. If I had to return those damn shoes, surely an island getaway is out.*

So fun. I just like Piers's confidence and free spirit. (By the way, Piers, I really fancy books and music, too.) Viewers respond well to our guest hosts. It's fun for them to watch people they're interested in reveal themselves outside of their comfort zones. It's also fun for me and Kathie Lee, because it shakes the show up a little, and then we look forward to getting back into our regular rhythm together.

The guests on our show are equally as intriguing. By far, the majority are kind and appreciative and gracious. Even after the cameras go dark. Some are accompanied by a slew of handlers and helpers, but most are not. Especially the big stars. They walk in only with their celebrity and their enthusiasm about the project they're promoting. I admit that I do get "pinch me" moments. Like the morning James Taylor and Carole King both sat down with us. Can you imagine? The soundtrack of my life sitting next to the other soundtrack. I tried my best not to make doe eyes and fawn over them. I did hug James Taylor at the end. I hugged him. I didn't care. I went in for the big one. Aretha Franklin, Sophia Loren, Shirley MacLaine, Queen Latifah—mindblowers. It's all weird. I gotta say. One morning Julie Andrews walked by in the hallway and I felt eight years old again. As I said earlier, it's not as intriguing for Kathie Lee because she's interviewed so many celebrities during her years on live TV. The only star I've seen KLG weak-kneed about was Kevin Costner. He got her good. She got really dressed up on that day.

Kathie Lee came up with the idea of inviting our moms on as guests from time to time to cook their favorite holiday recipes. Kathie Lee's mom, Joanie, decided one visit to prepare cottage cheese balls, while my mom chose garlic shrimp. Because it's too hard to complete a recipe during a short TV segment—especially for amateurs—the *Today* show has a kitchen guru named Bianca who prepares the featured food using the recipes supplied by the guests. Still, my mom was very nervous. "I don't know what to say!" she told me. I kept reassuring her, "Mom, it's Kathie Lee and her mother. We're not going to be able to get a word in edgewise. Don't worry." Both moms got their hair and makeup done by Laura and Mary. My mom wanted her look to be conservative. "Let's keep it light, okay? I don't want to be all glamorous." We had such a good time cooking with Sami and Joanie. They were great sports and did their best to follow instructions. I still crack up picturing them trying to go with the flow as we went to the

TODAY'S HOLIDAY KITCHEN
KATHIE LEE & HODA'S FAMILY DINNERS

TODAY   KLGandHODA.COM

A recipe for fun

first commercial break. The producers coached them to do *something* for the cameras as we "teased" what was coming up next. My mom smiled and fake-stirred the garlic shrimp, and Joanie began waving her hands in a circular motion, at a loss for something to do. They were hilarious and cute. After the show, people on the street actually stopped my mom to tell her how much they enjoyed her cooking segment. That was a thrill for her, but nothing topped the fact that Al Roker talked to her. Al is my mom's favorite and she basically stalks him when she's at NBC with me. "Al talked to me!" she'll report back. "Yes, Mom. Al is very nice." Kathie Lee and I love having our moms on the show. What's better than sharing your real family with your work family?

Larry King was a guest in May of 2009. The television and radio talk show legend had written a book titled *My Remarkable Journey*, and our fourth-hour set was a stop on his book tour. Apparently, in part of the book, Larry talks about his desire to be cryogenically preserved. Well, before the cameras even turned on, we gave him an idea of what that would be like in the here and now. The upstairs set of Studio 1A is an icebox. If we could, we'd wear earmuffs and parkas to combat the frigid temperatures. Unfortunately, that's where we put Larry as he waited for his segment, slated for the downstairs studio. His teeth were chattering when he finally joined us downstairs.

"What are you trying to do, friggin' *kill* me?" Larry yelled at us through blue lips.

Can't you just hear him saying that?

Thankfully, we ended up having fun with it. The whole segment became him accusing us of trying to "friggin' *off* him." I'm pretty sure his book got shortchanged. Now the barometer (or thermometer) for how cold the studio feels is measured on the LK index.

"God, it's *freezing* in here!" we'll say. "But not as cold as when we almost killed Larry King."

Kathie Lee and I both agree that one of our favorite interviews was Beyoncé. The twenty-eight-year-old superstar agreed to a taped interview the day after one of the biggest nights of her life. Hours earlier, Beyoncé had set a record for the most Grammy Award wins by a female artist in one night. On January 31, 2010, she took home six statues (after being nominated for ten) at the 52nd Annual Grammy Awards. Her hit song "Single Ladies (Put a Ring on It)" won Song of the Year. No doubt exhausted and heading out for the South American leg of her "I AM . . ." world tour, Beyoncé somehow made time to chat with us. We were given fifteen minutes. Our producers found an office building located near Union Square for the interview, and crews spent their usual two hours creating a beautiful temporary set for us.

When Beyoncé walked into the room, we were blown away by her beauty and presence. She's about 5 feet 7, but her red heels added several inches. She wore a gorgeous short dress, designed in her favorite color, red. She was a knockout. Her frame is sexy and solid and she carries herself with confidence around every curve. She dropped down into the chair with a friendly "Hey!" We most often hear Beyoncé's singing voice, so it was almost odd to hear her speak. Her words were laced with a touch of Texas twang. (Beyoncé was born and raised in Houston.) As her people began touching up her hair and makeup, all I could think was, *There's absolutely nothing wrong with her! Bring that stuff over here!*

From the minute Beyoncé sat down, there was something refreshing about her. There were no walls, no talking points, and no glazed look stars sometimes get from having to tell the same story a hundred times. Beyoncé simply brought herself. Because we had such a short amount of time, Kathie Lee and I got right into her Grammy Awards sweep the night before. In unison, we reeled off the list of female artists she'd out-Grammied, with her now total of sixteen.

"Barbra Streisand, eight. Tina Turner, eight," we marveled. "Celine Dion, five."

Beyoncé's beautiful jaw dropped. She was in shock.

"That is so scary" was her humble reaction.

We asked her how she could possibly stay so grounded while her world was so clearly in orbit.

"Being around my family keeps me grounded. My mother is a very special woman. She is very honest with me as well as my husband, and my female friends—we call ourselves the Blackbirds." She smiled. "It's great to know when I take off all the makeup and heels that I have a life and I have warmth and I have reality."

And you know what? We believed her. We could picture her at home, grabbing a handful of popcorn, just hanging out with the people she loves. We then asked her how she manages to stay out of the tabloids and protect her privacy with her rapper husband Jay-Z.

"I think I'm a little too busy!" she laughed. "I think I work so much that when I'm getting off the stage and I've given one hundred percent, all I want to do is go to the hotel, get in some UGGs, and watch television."

Beyoncé is a workhorse and I'm a sucker for that. I love anyone who's busting it to pursue his or her passion. She told us that when she's working on an album she misses acting. When she's doing a film, she's eager to record new music. "The longer you do something, the harder it is to top yourself and try to discover what you haven't done yet," she explained. "It's challenging to always try to grow and have your fans grow with you."

It was weird sitting across from Beyoncé because she is so normal and fun. We laughed about her watching a marathon of the TV show *The Jersey Shore* in her hotel room. It was so easy to lose sight of her superstardom. *Oh, Lord, it's Beyoncé!* I'd remind myself. A month earlier, she had launched her signature fragrance, Heat. (And why not, right? What else is she doing but singing, songwriting, producing records, acting, and modeling? Workhorse.) Kathie Lee had a bottle of Heat in her hand and commented about how sexy it looked and that the red and gold color combination mimicked the dress Beyoncé was wearing. The superstar said they were her two favorite colors and joked that the bottle was shaped like her.

"My figure's kind of like that," Beyoncé laughed. "Heavy at the bottom."

We loved her! And we could have stayed for an hour. Even Beyoncé seemed surprised when our fifteen minutes ended. "It's over?" she asked. We definitely experienced quality over quantity with her. That girl is impressive within ten seconds. I'm so glad I met Beyoncé in person. That makes my time with her on my iPod even more fun.

P.S.

How about this for a blast from the past? Some thirty-five years later, I got to meet the hunk from the poster on the back of my bedroom door. In April of 2010, Erik Estrada was a guest on the fourth hour of *Today*. How crazy is that? My junior high heartthrob in the flesh! Erik was so nice and gave me a big hug. He flashed that signature Ponch smile (his teeth are still really white!) just like I remember from the *CHiPs* days. He's now involved with a nationwide task force that hunts down sexual predators who prowl the Internet for kids. Three decades later, my guy fights crime for real!

21

THE PEACOCK FAMILY

Okay. Corny alert. But this is true: the people I work with feel like family. Matt, Al, Meredith, Ann, Natalie, the producers, and the crew are all top-notch. Sure, none of us is perfect, but these guys are perfectly wonderful to call colleagues. If you watch the *Today* show and get the sense that we like each other, you're right. There's no phoniness.

"That's right, Meredith [*fake smile and chuckle*]. So, tell us about the weather, Al [*cheesy wink; stiff turn to camera 1*]."

There's none of that.

We really *do* like each other. We know each other well, too. There's no way to avoid it—we're up at odd hours together when people's true colors come out, we spend 24/7 together on long trips covering the Olympics or other big news events, and there are daily deadlines, which tend to reveal character and attitude. After getting to know all these folks, I can honestly say there is a collective spirit of gratitude.

Everyone is thankful to work on the *Today* show and no one person feels like it's *my* show. It's *our* show.

I credit *Today* show executive producer Jim Bell for a lot of that "Go, Team" tone. Jim came to NBC News from NBC Olympics in 2005. He also played defensive tackle at Harvard. At 6 feet 4, 250 pounds, Jim is a commanding figure, but it's his watch that's the real power player. When you head up four hours of morning television, you'd better be able to fire off solid decisions under deadline pressure like a human Gatling gun. Jim does it exceptionally well. (Check our ratings.) Whenever I walk into his office, I make my point quickly. Bang-bang! Jim's tough, but as kind as they come. He's raising four boys and his strong and kind wife, Angelique, makes you love him even more. I'm grateful Jim's our leader, and I can't say enough for my teammates.

Meredith and Matt, seated; Steve Capus, Al, Jim Bell, Ann, and me

Every morning, Al Roker walks into the makeup room doing a song and dance. You never see a rain cloud around that guy. One February, Al and I flew to New Orleans to ride a float together in the Krewe of Argus Parade in Jefferson Parish. We rode on Fat Tuesday and did our show live from the parade route. This is going to sound ridiculous, but there's something exhilarating and exhausting about riding on a float. There's a lot of waiting, and then sudden yelling and connecting with hundreds of people. I don't know why, but it somehow wears you out. After the show, our flight home was delayed and we arrived back in New York City late in the evening.

Just a few hours later, I was sitting in the makeup chair like a zombie, getting ready for the show. In walked Al. "Hellllllooooooo. Look. it's Hoooooooooda!" he chirped. I couldn't believe it. He acted like he got a full night's sleep, when I know he slept for maybe two hours. I said to him, "How do you do it?" He answered through that huge smile, "Let me tell you why I'm happy. It's because my dad drove a city bus, and I get to come to 30 Rock every single day and work." That told me all I need to know about Al Roker. Done.

Again, that's the common thread at the *Today* show. A thread that stitches the word: *grateful*. All the people you watch have worked hard to get where they sit. No one had a gimme. Their investment of time and effort paid off, and because that doesn't always happen, they feel lucky. Matt is the perfect example of setting the right tone for the show. He's *always* polite and respectful. If he's dashing in to make a segment, there's no rudeness or abruptness with the crew. "Excuse me, Antoine. I'm sorry, I just have to get in here," he'll say, moving through the bodies. He's also one of the funniest people I know and one of the most considerate. Matt was the first person who called me when I got out of the recovery room after my breast cancer surgery.

Matt, Meredith, Ann, Al, and Natalie are asked to pop around the globe, often at a moment's notice. You *never* hear any of them complain about being tired or away from their families. They just go, and do, and do it again. One morning in the makeup room, I knew Matt had just gotten back from some Timbuktu-ish place and I asked him when he got back. "Oh, around midnight." That meant: somewhere between midnight and six o'clock in the morning, Matt arrived back home, studied for all his segments, slept?, and came into work. I'm not saying talent doesn't earn the dollars to do it, it's just the consistent good attitude that I find priceless. Even the crew members who are up all night prepping the *Today* show sets *always* greet me with, "Good morning, Hoda!" They'll yell from atop a ladder, "How was your night?" I've been there long enough now to know that all the goodwill is genuine. It's just a fun place to work.

The person who makes me laugh every day is Meredith. In the name of decorum, I can't share half the things she says, but trust me— the woman is brilliant. In February of 2008, *Today* took the show on the road for a "Fire and Ice" special. We broadcast shows from chilly Warren, Vermont, then flew to hot Miami for shows there. Thankfully, we all got stuck in Florida due to travel delays up north. The whole gang was happily trapped and we spent the afternoon soaking up sun by the pool and enjoying some cocktails.

As we sat around a table, I blurted out, "Oh, my gosh. I *have* to tell you this funny story about my watch!" Well, that's like chumming the water for Meredith's sense of humor. She immediately stood up and yelled to everyone, waving her arms, "Hold the phone, everybody! Hoda has a really"—her fingers do air quotes—"*interesting* story about her watch!" Then to the pool waiter, "Excuse me, we're gonna need some double shots, because she's about to tell a really (air quotes again) *interesting* story about her watch that went missing." I was laughing so hard I could barely tell the tale of how a guy with a metal detector found my watch. That *is* interesting, right?!

For laughs, Meredith. For energy, Ann Curry. When that woman walks into the makeup room, the energy meter spikes. She should be called Amp Curry. Ann has an energy source that she can focus like a laser beam, and she uses it when she talks to people. Whether it's an interview on the couch, or a face in the crowd, or a colleague in the makeup chair, she's 110 percent interested.

"So, how ya doin'?" she'll say to me in the morning, as I'm sitting in the makeup chair. I'll glance over at the clock and see that she's one minute away from her newscast.

"Did that thing go okay for you last night?" she'll continue.

"Yep." I'll say, chopping my answer. "Ann, you have one minute."

"Okay. But you're good?"

She really does want to know.

No one loves what she does more than Ann. Especially the pursuit of a story. If you were to offer her the option of anchoring the news or chasing a story, she'd be out the door in a second. Always. For as beautiful and put-together as she is on air, Ann is the first one to be wandering the halls without makeup after the show. She's the comfy gal, the jeans-and-T-shirt gal. And throw in a pair of Energizer Bunny slippers.

Perhaps the nicest person I know at NBC is Natalie Morales. She's the kind of girl who's *so* pretty that women want to hate her. But no one can, because she's so damn nice. Natalie sees the good side of everybody. She's also smart and her world is organized. Everything's highlighted, underlined, and neatly stacked.

"What *is* that?" I'll ask her.

Ladies' night: Ann Curry, Melissa Lonner, me, Bobbie Thomas,
Natalie Morales, Tammy Filler

"Oh, just my segments," she'll say, completely on top of everything.

I don't know where she finds the time—juggling work, two kids, and a husband. The great thing about Natalie is, you can also throw her into any random situation and she's just as good. She handles it all beautifully. But one warning: Natalie is fiercely competitive when it comes to athletics. The girl can burn it up! When *Self* magazine asked us to compete in a triathlon, Natalie ranked in the top three of her age group. I barely finished. I'd put my money on Natalie any day.

Like I warned you, corny alert—but, when it comes to my *Today* show family, I'm as proud as a peacock.

22

DATING

No one thinks that at age forty-four, they'll be dating again. Oh, well. We never think our metabolism will shut off like a faucet, either. Dating again is weird. That's the long and short of it. For so many years, I spent mornings, nights, and weekends with the same man. I kissed the same man. We finally figured out our sleep numbers. All the legwork was behind me—and then, "So, where did you grow up? Do you have brothers and sisters?" I'm starting again from ground zero.

After my divorce in early 2008, the thought of dating again was not even a consideration for quite a while. My marriage was over well before all the papers were signed, so I guess it took me almost a full year before I was open to meeting men. Initially, I didn't want to date a man who'd been married before. But then I decided that wasn't a good idea, for two reasons: (1) at my age that shrinks the pool down to a small puddle, and (2) I determined that instead, I wanted to make sure I was with a guy who had a track record of commitment.

A man should have some history of a long-term relationship (not necessarily marriage)—an ability to share his life. Having a second shot at a partner certainly makes you think about what you want this time around. I actually wrote down the three traits that were most important to me and tucked the paper into an envelope. I stashed it in a wooden box handmade by country singer Jo Dee Messina's woodworking whiz husband—something special inside something special. I planned to open it when I met Mr. Right. You know what? I can't even remember what I wrote down. Someday, I'll read it and smile. I'll bet I show him, too.

When I finally did decide to dunk my baby toe in the dating waters, I was cautious. You know how it is. Someone breaks your heart and your trust, so you put up walls. Even though you shouldn't, you see flashing danger signs all over the person sitting across the table. Some of the walls around me were fortified with bra straps. Dating after breast reconstruction includes added anxiety about "the Big Reveal." Or in my case, "the Small Reveal." Clearly, by our forties, we've got personal baggage and so do the people we date. Love after forty requires an additional skill: baggage handler.

Here's another dilemma—where the hell do you meet people? I don't go to bars, I rarely grocery shop, and I am at the gym solely to exercise. I'm also not an Internet gal. My mom, on the other hand, is apparently in "eligible guy" hot spots constantly. "I met the nicest guy on the train for you!" she told me one day, very excited. Oh, Lord. She got his phone number *and* showed him my picture! I met him for coffee and that was it. Look, the minute my mom stops doing that I'm really in trouble because that means she's given up hope.

The starting place for me to meet people actually turned out to be small parties thrown by friends. I liked the idea of that—safe surroundings, reputable crowd, easy exit. I met some very nice men but nothing serious. Then, in April of 2009, our *Today* show producers booked the Kellehers. Jill Kelleher and Amber Kelleher-Andrews are a mother-daughter team who run Kelleher & Associates, a high-end matchmaking service with a twenty-plus-year track record. They were the stars of our "Matchmaking Series," featuring singles from our viewing audience who agreed to be set up. Producers asked me if I'd be interested in getting "match-made" on the air as well. Sure! Why not? The Kellehers claimed an 85 percent success rate, and they were going to do all the legwork. Basically, the ladies conduct intensive interviews with both sides of the match and pair people who they feel share common ground. I would go on two dates with the guy they selected for me, and talk about the experience on the show. For me, the Kellehers selected a tall, handsome British bloke named John. He flew in from California to go on our dates. Good-looking and good-sounding with a suave English accent, John was impressive. I was looking forward to getting to know him better. So was Kathie Lee. She called it Frank's "sniff test." Kathie Lee wanted me to bring John over to her house for dinner as our first date so Frank could check him out. Fine. I love Frank, so why wouldn't I want him to get "nosey" about my dating life? And so, in May, John and I went to the Giffords for a casual, fun dinner for our first evening together. We had a lot of laughs and I enjoyed his company. Frank seemed okay with him, but a few hours are not sufficient for a true read. The next evening, we planned to go to Mr. Chow, an upscale Chinese restaurant in Manhattan. John was sweet and brought me a dozen roses. (What would my fortune cookie say?) Dinner was enjoyable and it was nice to feel some chemistry again with a man. Afterward, we took a romantic carriage ride through Central Park. The next morning on the show, John joked that he had half-expected Kathie Lee to jump out of the bushes in the park. Turns out, in the end, John was not as available as we thought. He was already involved with someone at the time. But it was fun to meet him and I began to look forward to all those second "firsts"—the first handhold, the first hug, the first kiss.

Five months later, our producers booked Diana Kirschner— psychologist, relationship expert, and author of the book *Love in 90 Days*. Three months? Tell us more. Diana's theory makes sense. Her drill is to meet three guys, date them, let them know you're dating other people, and don't sleep with them. The concept is to develop a sampling of personalities, then recognize the traits that truly matter to you. Don't complicate it with sex, and avoid the waiting-by-the-phone-for-one-person syndrome. Off the air, I met with Diana and came up with her requested "Mission Statement." I'm going to keep that private, in case my mission changes. For several months, I followed the program and enjoyed the process. Go wide, not deep. I did not find love in ninety days, but in defense of Diana's theory, I didn't do a good job of following all the rules. No, *not* the sex part; just the dating of three different people. All the time required for that seemed too hard to carve out. I still think about Diana's theory when I date now and appreciate her planting some very helpful seeds.

"When am I taking you to dinner?" A gorgeous guy I met at a literacy fundraiser came out with that line. I loved his confidence. There really is a lot to like about the dating process. Picking out the right outfit, feeling those once-grounded butterflies again, wondering if you'll get a good-night kiss. Certain things never go away, no matter how old you get. Neither do the shitty dates. I've already had my share of disappointments. (Granted, I may have doled out a few myself.) During a double date I was on with a girlfriend, my guy never reached for the check when it hit the table. Didn't even flinch. He said, "Why don't we let the ladies pay?" I prefer a gentleman. On another date, my suitor began eating his meal before mine even arrived. Really? A pet might do that, but a man should not. There have been times when I've wanted to leave in the middle of a date or even at the beginning. I couldn't get my key in the front door fast enough. Again, I may have caused the same reaction for my date. That's just how it is. I try to roll with it all. I also keep in mind *not* to put the sins of my former guy on guys I meet now. I don't want to see the bogeyman in everyone. That's not fair and it's not real, either.

I have to admit I have developed a question to speed up the dating process a bit. It may be a turnoff, but oh, well. I just feel like there's so much time wasted trying to disarm the on-my-best-behavior person to get to the real person. If only we were all truthful from the start!

So, here's the question I sometimes ask men I've been dating for a few weeks: "If I lined up all the women you've had significant relationships with, what would *they* all say is the common reason the relationship didn't work?"

Pretty good, right? The answer is telling. It underscores a relationship "pattern."

One man told me—and I applaud his honesty—this: "I go after women until they fall in love with me and then I break up with them."

Check, please!

Another man admitted—and again, I applaud his honesty—this: "I'm always looking for the next thing." (He did say he's changed now.)

Always, they return the question, which is only fair.

My answer is this: "They'd say I didn't need them enough."

It's true. I'm just not needy. But I think part of that is not being able to trust someone. I'm clearly a work in progress. I honestly feel zero panic (Kathie Lee). I'm a true believer in healing followed by hope. I do want to get married again. I like the idea of sharing my life with a good man. I'm better with someone else. He'll have to have infinite patience with me and be there for me. My guy will stand the test of time and stand tall doing it.

Hmm . . . what *did* I write in that letter I stashed away?

23

FORWARD

What better way to wrap up my book than with a look *forward*. To the future. As you now know in my life (and probably in your own), there's just no telling what's coming next. In a way, that's good. Would any one of us get up in the morning if we knew about some of the shit storms headed our way?

I'm not a horoscope girl or a believer in otherworldly stuff, but in January of 2009, *Today* show fashion editor Bobbie Thomas gave me a unique gift. Bobbie's a big fan of an astrologer named Carol Cummings, so she booked me an hourlong astrology reading with Carol, whose email address begins *cosmic.carol*. Now, "cosmic" to me means fun, not fact. So, I agreed to hear Carol's predictions as a lighthearted adventure—a trip to the cosmos then back to my earthly existence. Before we spoke by phone, Carol asked me to email my birth time and date and other personal stats for her to plug into various celestial charts. She then mailed me a forty-page report detailing my Life and Soul Mission. (Forty pages?! Does the Mission come with staff?) Our one-hour follow-up phone call was to review the findings and discuss what was ahead for me. Fun, right?

And it was. Carol could not have been nicer and told me up front that she had a very good track record after twenty-five years of astrological readings. "I'm not one hundred percent right, but I'm right about eighty-five percent of the time," she explained.

What did I have to lose? My Mission would be revealed, and then I'd get back to discussing the art of "flirtexting" with Kathie Lee and two guests.

Because listening to someone else's astrological reading is like watching someone else's vacation videos ("Your fifth house is very busy and Pluto is opposing Venus . . ."), I'll spare you the details.

Here's a synopsis of what I took away from the experience:

1. I'm apparently a Double Leo. *Finally, an explanation for this hair.*
2. At fifty-nine, I will finally realize how I've helped society evolve. *Plenty of time to find the perfect dress.*
3. There is a very important love relationship in my near future to make up for all the loneliness in my past lives. *Oh, darn, that will obliterate ninety percent of Kathie Lee's material.*
4. I'm destined to write more books. *Note to self: highlight and fax to publisher.*

Overall, it was an intriguing way to spend an hour. I appreciated Bobbie's gift and Carol's passion. I've now moved on with my daily doings, far below the blanket of stars that hold the "answers" to my future.

I really don't worry about what's ahead. My measure of the "future" is more day-to-day than year-to-year. Scratch the five-year plan—I prefer to create mini milestones to skip across uncharted waters. Thinking any deeper is pointless and takes away from focusing on the good ol' present. My crystal ball is calibrated for short-term hopes and dreams: a sunny morning, a beach vacation circled in red on my calendar, the thump-thump of chemistry with a man.

As you read this, I'm probably having a good day. That's not to say some aren't frustrating, but on most given days, I feel lucky. I've learned not to sweat the small stuff because when I look around, my "stuff" is pretty damn small. I *try* to remember that daily, even on mornings when I've got the gum wad ready for Kathie Lee's hair.

Here's another little gem I've unearthed in recent years. You *can't* resolve everything in your life. Stop with the four-hour phone calls and lunches, burning through hours dissecting a stubborn issue. I think it's okay to tuck some things away and live your life. *Stop* wishing for a resolution! Life's not perfect. Some loose ends may never get trimmed up and tidied. I believe that and boy, it's freeing.

I've learned that another waste of time is waffling over decisions. Flip-flop tick-tock. What a time suck! I try not to look back after I make a big decision. I make my choice and then I move forward. If I can't sleep, I'll revisit it, but otherwise I sleep like a baby—who's made an adult decision.

Am I on the right path in my life? I think so. I really do. For the past few years, the dominoes have not only lined up, they've knocked each other down in that beautiful "effect" that opens door after door. Turns out, when you're on the right path, opportunities begin to unfold along the way. My rule now is that if I truly believe in something, I should go for it with gusto. I've discovered the power of not only positive thinking, but positive *doing*. Do it and watch those dominoes fall—plink-plink-plink-plink.

I've always had a solid foundation for a good life—my family and close friends I can count on one hand. My focus now is creating quality blueprints to build my next forty years. I'm excited, hopeful, open, and ready for all the challenges that come with a work in progress. You can't scare me, but you can definitely make me laugh. I'm going to stockpile as much laughter and joy as I can for the rest of my life.

Well, I'm down to the last blueberry. Whatever I've forgotten has simply missed its shot at greatness. What I *won't* forget is sharing my journey with you. Thank you for that. I leave you with the same advice I wish someone had given me years ago: start writing things down.

WHERE ARE THEY NOW?

Hmm. Where are they now? Where are some of the people (and things) who shaped my life and filled the pages of this book? I thought it would be fun to follow up on a few with fresh news and photos. The Internet sure makes it easy to track people down. Right, Jon Zachman?

I list them in order of how you met each other in *HODA*.

Jon Zachman (basement makeout boy), *page 16*: My junior high makeout buddy was "history" when he heard my parents come home from work early! How perfect, then, that Jon grew up to become the curator of collections at the Greensboro Historical Museum in North Carolina.

Peggy Fox (friend who left class to sit by duck pond), *page 24*: My loyal friend Peggy graduated from Virginia Tech and began her career as a television journalist. She now works at WUSA-TV in Washington, D.C., as a news reporter. Peggy has a son and daughter and loves being a mom. She and I see each other once a year to catch up on the news biz, and the news of our lives.

Hannah (my three-year-old niece), *page 28*: Hannah is still as adorable as ever! She loves to be read to and Dora the Explorer is her girl. She's crazy for broccoli and my mom's meatballs, and, of course, her Aunt Hodie.

Laura Castorino (my hair angel), *page 44*: Laura is right where she should be—at the ready with her magic round brush. She recently got her own new hairstyle, but her husband's not a fan. He claims that Laura looks like Keith Partridge and belts out "I Think I Love You." I think he's in big trouble.

Stan Sandroni (first news director), *page 53*: Stan doesn't age! He is now an account executive for a telecommunications company in Oxford, Mississippi. Still a sports fanatic, Stan's also the sideline reporter for the Ole Miss Rebel Football Network.

Aung San Suu Kyi (held under house arrest in Burma), *page 76*: She remains under house arrest in Burma. In March of 2010, the high court

denied her request for an appeal, rendering her unable to participate in the November elections. Activists and freedom-loving people across the world continue to push for Aung San Suu Kyi's release.

Ms. Groves (first-time teacher), *page 100*: After two years of teaching at Atlanta's Jean Childs Young Middle School, Monica left to go back to school herself. She completed her master's degree in teaching and curriculum through Harvard's Teacher Education Program. Monica then returned to Jean Childs Young to teach eighth-grade English, where she currently works. In 2011, Monica will become dean at KIPP Vision Academy, also in Atlanta.

Moss Man (twirled me at Mardi Gras), *page 115:* My surprise dance partner at Mardi Gras 1992 was the huggable, tuggable Moss Man. Sadly he passed away in 2004, but leaves behind a legacy of

thrilling Mardi Gras crowds for nearly two decades. New Orleanians still ask me what I thought when he swept me off my feet that morning. Moss Man is not forgotten.

My iPod, *page 156*: Where *is* it now? I think someone "borrowed" one of my iPods from the gym! I'm down to one, but not for long. I'm going to buy a backup and a backup to the backup, too.

Man on the Plane ("Don't hog your journey"), *page 183* My man on the plane is doing well, but, ironically, had a cancer scare. In 2009, Ken Duane was diagnosed with prostate cancer and successfully underwent treatment. I was so grateful when he called to share *his* journey with me.

Eduardo Verástegui (star of *Bella*), *page 216*: We're *still* not married! Eduardo's busy pursuing movies and music. He also travels the world promoting life and family. Eduardo's heart is even more beautiful than his being, which makes me love him even more.

My special wooden box (holds letter that lists the three most important traits in my man), *page 256*: It's in my guest bedroom on a

bookshelf. Writing this down will help me find that little box one day when I need it. As you now know, there's a chance it will end up accidentally buried by books, an oversized tote bag, a plaque, or other random crap.

ACKNOWLEDGMENTS

I have a lousy track record when it comes to writing thank-you notes, but not this time. There are too many people who added huge value to this book and I need to say thanks. (I'm also afraid of some of these people.)

In no particular order, I want to acknowledge:

David Rosenthal and Kerri Kolen at Simon & Schuster. From the start, I loved your combination of smart-ass and smart. You know which one you are. I'm grateful for the time, attention, and guidance you offered throughout the writing process. You simply let me be me. (Except for this paragraph, which you guys faxed to me and made me include.)

Also at Simon & Schuster: Aileen Boyle, Leah Wasielewski, Nina Pajak, Kate Ankofski, Jackie Seow, Victoria Meyer, and Brian Ulicky.

Mel Berger, my book agent, I just want to hug you. The minute I met you, I didn't care what we did together; I just wanted to be associated with you. Your reputation is gold and so is your heart. You are the most humble, health-conscious, easygoing rock star I know. I'm your biggest fan.

Kathie Lee, you lent me your veteran author expertise, your Florida home, and your name for this book. What can I say? And actually, why should I? After all, you're not going to read my book because you think I didn't read yours. Just in case you do read it, thank you for your love and loyalty. You're the best.

And finally to Jane—the most brilliant writer I have ever known. Your dad was right. It has been an adventure, although we did make one mistake. Your name should be bigger on the cover. Oh, well . . . next book.